ALEKSANDR SOLZHENITSYN

A Biography

ALEKSANDR SOLZHENITSYN

A Biography

Hans Björkegren

Translated from the Swedish
by Kaarina Eneberg

THE THIRD PRESS

JOSEPH OKPAKU PUBLISHING COMPANY, INC.
444 CENTRAL PARK WEST, NEW YORK, N.Y. 10025

92
5692 b

Library of Congress Catalogue Card Number: LC 72-80185
SBN 89388-050-7   T 18

Designed by Bennie Arrington

First printing

Translated from the Swedish
original: *Alexander Solsjenitsyn*
by Hans Björkegren copyright ©
1971 by Wahlstrom & Widstrand

Contents

INTRODUCTION	1
Childhood and Youth	5
Solzhenitsyn's War	21
The Imprisonment	27
Freedom	37
The Rehabilitation	39
The Debut	43
The Controversy Starts	49
The Fight About the Lenin Prize	63
International Controversies	67
The Invisible Front	73
The 23rd Party Congress	79
Cancer Ward is "Approved"	83
The Fourth Congress of Soviet Writers	87
Central Directives	119
The War of the Agents	123
The Pirate Editions	133
The Fiftieth Anniversary	135
An "Interview"	137
The Purge	141
The Isolation	161
The Nobel Prize	165
Bibliography	181
Index	183

INTRODUCTION

There he was, suddenly. So self-evident and monolithic and with a message so central that his appearance caused an immediate polarization.

Alexander Solzhenitsyn's debut with *One Day in the Life of Ivan Denisovich* was not, primarily, a result of the general relaxation in cultural politics which had been going on intermittently since the "thaw" in 1956 and was particularly noticeable in the months following the 22nd Party Congress in 1961. His appearance was the consequence of a political decision which was preceded by an obviously very bitter controversy among the top leaders. It was all in line with the politics of power, the details of which will, perhaps for ever, remain unclear or unknown.

The publication of *One Day in the Life of Ivan Denisovich* came after a year of obviously growing optimism among especially two intellectual factions. One of these groups consisted of the younger intellectuals whom the poet Yevgeni Yevtushenko, once called "the generation of the 20th Party Congress" (that is, of the de-Stalinization era). The other consisted of the older intellectuals (sometimes called "the Patrons") who called for a return to the "Golden Age" of Soviet culture, the nineteen twenties, when Lenin and his followers showed relative tolerance for artistic pluralism and experimental art. This was the decade of Meyerhold, Mikhoels, Tatlin, Mayakovsky and the Akmeists.

Especially after the end of 1961, that is to say, immediately after the 22nd Party Congress, these "liberals" had advanced their positions and were consolidating their ranks in the following spring and summer. Their growing influence was evident

1

in their organizations, in the movie councils, the exhibition committees, the publishing houses and on the editorial staff of the publications. They were encouraged by distinguished scholars, particularly by scientists, who arranged avant-garde exhibitions and lectures at "closed" and "semi-closed" institutions like the Kurchatov Institute in Moscow and "the Cities of Science"—Dubna, Novosibirsk and Obninsk. They travelled abroad and debated the fundamentals of culture to a much greater extent than before. They were trusted by the Party leadership, at least to some degree, and in any case, as long as it was consistent with Nikita Khrushchev's special political aspirations.

Several of them saw a spokesman for their cause in the Party leader's son-in-law, Alexei Adzhubei, at that time the editor of the government newspaper *Izvestia* and a member of the Central Committee. Also, they were tolerated by the more moderate elements in the Party apparatus and in the Ministry of Culture.

After, the new massive attacks on Joseph Stalin and the "Party Enemies" (Molotov, Kaganovich, Voroshilov and several others) at the 22nd Party Congress, the hard-core dogmatists seemed to be on the defensive in the cultural sector. Some of them made a tactical *volte-face,* among them Vsevold Kochetov, who in his magazine *Okchabr (October)* now published several articles that at least seemed to be critical of the society and to have an anti-Stalinist tendency.

Toward the summer of 1962 the dogmatists had apparently been forced back along the whole line and were now only trying to save the personal privileges such as dachas, higher salaries, trips abroad, and committee functions that they enjoyed.

However, these personal liberties seemed to be curtailed, and there were even signs and rumors indicating that several of the most notorious informers among the writers during the period of terror under Stalin (among them the critic Jakov Elsberg) had reason to fear for their lives. At this time, the younger intellectuals discussed reports—probably rather naive ones—claiming that the KGB or Security Police had begun a survey of "dogmatic, neo-Stalinist" elements, particularly people who could be suspected of "pro-Chinese" sympathies.

Whether they were founded or not, these rumors clearly indicate the atmosphere that prevailed at this time.

Early in the fall, Nikita Khrushchev was evidently preparing for a new step in the so-called de-Stalinization campaign. Highly-placed intellectuals in Moscow maintained that a new group of "Party Enemies" was about to be unmasked. This group was almost identical with the faction that seized power in the Communist Party in the fall of 1964. There were rumors of coming literary sensations such as the poetry of Osip Mandelshtam, the publication of whose works had been repeatedly postponed since the mid-fifties, previously unpublished (and probably deliberately ignored) documents by Anatoli Lunacharsky—the information commissar under Lenin—and controversial works by writers like Vladimir Mayakovsky, Maxim Gorky, Boris Pasternak, Anna Akhmatova and Boris Pilnyak. Strong forces were at work arranging art exhibitions of the works of Vasily Kandinsky, Marc Chagall and Vladimir Tatlin. In economic circles there was talk of a forth-coming modified "NEP"—the "New Economic Policy" modified in the spirit of the Kharkov Professor, Yevsei Liberman, and simply called "neo-NEP".

But it was soon obvious that the retreat of the "dogmatists" was only tactical and more in line with the formula "one step forward and two back." They were gathering their forces and it was obvious that their techniques, which had strong conspiratorial characteristics, were not only parallel, but evidently closely connected, with the aspirations of leading politicians to remove Khrushchev. They planned to launch another offensive over the entire political front shortly before the turn of the year 1962. They intended to take advantage of two simultaneous art shows as a pretext to demonstrate how strong they actually were and what an overwhelming political "barrage" they could count on from almost the entire Establishment. Behind them stood, in fact, extremely influential officials within the Party leadership, the Party apparatus, the Secret Police (KGB), Glavlit (the censorship agency), the military leadership and the bureaucracy.

It was to take these forces only two years to grow strong enough to sweep away Khrushchev and get even with his liberalization efforts. After the 22nd Party Congress Khrushchev, who had less support than was generally assumed, had begun to act more autocratically and without regard to the powerful Party apparatus. Defying the party statutes and the constitution, he started to split up the Party apparatus in the provinces into so-called industrial and agricultural committees. This project would, under any circumstances, have had great political consequences even if its purpose in the long run still remains unclear today. There is no doubt that the Party hierarchy considered it a threat, even as the embryo of a system of political factions. A similar tendency was noticeable in certain statements by Nikita Khrushchev about *One Day in the Life of Ivan Denisovich* and also in his efforts to get the book published over the heads of the censors.

Those threatened preferred to start out on the periphery, and from there, eat their way into the real heart of power. Shortly before the end of the year they had an excellent opportunity to strike out against the two most active "liberal" movements: the young intellectuals who were then advocating a *rapprochement* with Western aesthetic values, and the older generation who were fighting for a rehabilitation of the nineteen twenties and "modernism."

The attack against the old generation was launched in connection with a retrospective exhibition at the Manège—the central exhibition hall in Moscow—organized to celebrate the thirtieth anniversary of Moscow's Artists' Union. The central figure of this group was Ilya Ehrenburg who, since 1960, had been publishing his controversial memoirs *Men, Years, Life,* in issue after issue of the magazine, *Novy Mir*. In the light of the new liberalism, the exhibition committee had started to "rehabilitate" several older, previously controversial artists and movements for which Ehrenburg had been a controversial spokesman.

The blow against the younger generation was, however, struck at the simultaneously arranged "abstractionist" show in Elya Belutin's studio on Bolchaya Kommunisticheskaya Ulitsa in Moscow. This exhibition centered on sculptures and sketches by Ernst Neizvestny. The rest of the exhibits consisted of works by young painters of the most varied schools, but all had one common denominator: the denunciation of "social realism" in its traditional form. Several exhibitions of non-conformist art had been held before (and are still arranged) but the interesting fact about this one was that the organizers and visitors had, or had been given, the impression that they had the blessing of the district's Party and Komsomol officials.

Any action taken against the exhibition, and in particular against Ernst Neizvestny, could easily be extended to include his literary friends and followers, among them such controversial poets as Yevgeny Yevtushenko, Andrei Voznesensky, Robert Rozhdestvensky, Boris Slutsky, and the writer Victor Nekrasov. These men all had a compassion for experimental art combined with strong anti-Stalinist feelings and a personal involvement in social changes, which brought them closer to Ehrenburg's generation and the circle around Tvardovsky's magazine, Novy Mir.

Certain facts indicate that Khrushchev was "lured" to the Manège exhibition without being informed in advance of its unique character. He came there in an excellent mood, but eventually frowned at what he saw. He was also irritated by a group of art professors, who constantly whispered comments in his ear. Khrushchev was shaken by everything that did not correspond with his own rustic ideas about what art should be like. He was especially provoked by Robert Falk's cubistic deformations. His guides, the professors, took advantage of his disenchantment and especially pointed out works by young artists which had been rushed there from the abstract exhibition in Belutin's studio. There was a particularly bitter confrontation with Ernst Neizvestny, who defended his sculptures with desperate candor until he lost patience and suddenly shouted:

"You may be the Premier as much as you like, but in front

of my works I'm the Premier and we should talk on equal terms!"

The incident is referred to correctly by John Berger in his book about Neizvestny, *Art and Revolution*.

Nikita Khrushchev evidently did not suspect that he was on his way right into a political quagmire when striking out against "the modernistic pseudo-art" and "the clown art", to mention only some of the terms he used.

The dogmatists were united and ready for a fight. They had mobilized their supporters in the mass media and thereby forced a debate which first only dealt with artistic ways of expression and the behavior of individual writers during their trips abroad. The debate quickly expanded to the broader aspects of cultural politics, and finally, the entire ideological complex, including the attitude to Stalin, "the experienced methods" and the fundamentals of the Establishment.

In 1961 there had been some private discussions on a remarkable anthology, *Pages from Tarusa*. The book was edited by Konstantin Paustovsky and included works by writers and artists connected with the "Cultural Village" of Tarusa, not far from Lev Tolstoy's Yasnaya Polyana.

Several of the pieces were controversial, among them short stories by Yuri Kazakov, poems by Boris Slutsky and the pacifistic, anti-heroic novel *Good Luck Fellow,* by the almost legendary protest singer Bulat Okudzhava. The book had already been set to type by a printing shop in the provincial town of Kaluga when word came that it could not be distributed.

Paustovsky was very anxious to get the book released. The anthology was obviously regarded as a test case by certain circles—at least that was the impression of representatives involved with the two "liberal" groups: Ehrenburg's generation of the twenties and Yevtushenko's followers of the fifties. It is most likely that Khrushchev was aware of this when he personally intervened in the spring of 1962 and ordered the distribution of the volume to the bookstores. His action, which many people in Moscow knew of, was interpreted as an invitation to the "liberals" to join Khrushchev's efforts. But shortly afterwards the anthology was withdrawn from the market.

For some time there had been some kind of a second "re-habilitation" of controversial Soviet classics. Evidence of this could be seen in the Tarusa Anthology which included Paustovsky's personal notes on Ivan Bunin, Yuri Olyesha and Vladimir Lugovskoi, as many as forty-two poems by Marina Tsvetaeva, poems by Nikolai Zabolotsky and articles by the theatre leader Vsevolod Meyerhold. Books published at the end of that decade included works by emigrants such as Bunin, Kuprin and Tsvetaeva as well as works by "the domestic emigrants" Akhmatova, Pasternak and Zoshchenko and by "the forgotten" Andrei Platonov and Mikhail Bulgakov. The publication *The Day of Poetry, 1962* carried poems by Velemir Khlebnikov, Akhmatova, Pasternak, Osip Mandelshtam and Zabolotsky. The first volume of *A Short Encyclopedia of Literature* was published at the beginning of 1962. This first volume (Aarne to Gavrilov), which was strongly criticized later, was actually a true mass rehabilitation of writers, who had been repressed under Stalin's rule, and of emigrants and other disputed publicists. The same trend was noticeable in the movie industry, in theater, and in art.

The elation of a break-through, of normalization and of a new freedom grew stronger among both groups. The gigantic Lenin stadium—Luzhniki—in Moscow was frequently open to the young poets (Yevtushenko, Voznesensky, Okudzhava, Rozhestvensky and Bella Akhmadulina) who gathered around the magazine *Yunost*. These nights of poetry reading on a large scale were actually a revival of a tradition of the twenties, the days of Mayakovsky and Yesenin. They had a surprisingly strong public impact and soon developed into ideological manifestations. These young people were advocating a kind of "neo-Marxism" which the dogmatists found easy to dismiss as "revisionism." They were anxious to stress a historical and emotional connection between the ideals of the revolution and the young generation, between the twenties and the fifties. These nights which were dominated by the young poets were always attended by a "liberal" representative of the old generation which included intellectuals like Ilya Ehrenburg, Pavel Antokolsky, and Stepan Shchipachov.

The magazine *Yunost* experienced a rebuff with the resignation of the editor, Valentin Katayev, one of the great and original writers of the old generation. He was succeeded by Boris Polevoi, who, despite his unfavorable reputation, undoubtedly continued and even extended the "liberal" policy of Katayev, particularly, the relationship between the generation of the twenties and the young poets. In addition, the ration of newsprint to the magazine was increased—a clear indication that the authorities did not have a negative attitude. Toward the end of 1962 the circulation of this monthly magazine exceeded half a million while the staff estimated its actual readership at nearly two million. As a consequence of this young writers such as Yevtushenko and Aksyonov were brought into the editorial management, and this gave it a "liberal" inclination—even though the power of the so-called Editorial Council was only nominal. There were already other "liberals," among them the playwright Viktor Rozov and the Jewish poet Samuil Marshak. In any case, *Yunost* soon appeared as a "liberal" voice together with *Novy Mir*.

There were persistent rumors in Moscow that Khrushchev was planning some kind of a "new phase" for the summer in the de-Stalinization campaign and needed the support of gifted "liberal" publicists. The intervention by the head of the Party on behalf of the Tarusa Anthology, Yevtushenko's poem "The Heirs of Stalin" and particularly, Solzhenitsyn's debut story, seemed to confirm these rumors. In any case, it is a fact that Khrushchev, during that summer, was in contact with leading figures connected with *Novy Mir,* particularly Aleksandr Tvardovsky. Ever since the 22nd Party Congress when Tvardovsky attracted great attention with his famous speech he had maintained the status of "poet laureate" of the regime, for some time even outshining Sholokov. Tvardovsky's own poems were sacrosanct and he combined the job as the dynamic editor of *Novy Mir* with that of a prominent official of the Writers' Union, and at the same time was a supplicant for a seat on the Central Committee.

The contacts with Khrushchev had already produced some

effect by the early fall. On September 21 Tvardovsky was able to authorize the printing of the November issue of *Novy Mir,* acting on a preliminary promise by Khrushchev.

But it may be asked why it took the anonymous censor A06787 until November 3 to approve of the magazine.

During this period of waiting Khrushchev took action. Proof-sheets of Solzhenitsyn's story had been sent out to all members of the Party Presidium and to some trusted members of the Writers' Union. Khrushchev had hinted that the writer had to fight for the publication. He maintained that the story had to be published without any obstruction by the censors, that is, over the heads of the censors on Glavlit. A more or less rebellious group within the Presidium voiced a variety of different opinions ranging from various alterations to a total ban.

In this way, Aleksandr Solzhenitsyn's sixty-three-page story, *One Day in the Life of Ivan Denisovich,* caused a political polarization of the top Party leadership. Unfortunately, it is not known which of the Party leaders sided with Solzhenitsyn from the very beginning. Khrushchev's personal attitude was frank and absolutely clear: *One Day in the Life of Ivan Denisovich* was, as he later declared, "truthful and written with Party principles in mind."

By mid-October Khrushchev had carried his will through. There is hardly any reason to believe that his main motive was the concern for a new, great literary talent; for, during his years in power, Khrushchev had many times demonstrated a persistent lack of sensibility in cultural matters. This was obvious during the cultural crisis of 1956 and during the dispute over Vladimir Dudintsev's novel *Not By Bread Alone.* His motives were now, as before, only part of a scheme in a power game, and he had no genuine concern for the art of literature.

It was at this time that Yevgeni Yevtushenko also appeared on the scene. He too had been in contact with officials in the circle around the Party leader in the summer and fall. More sensitive than most people to the atmosphere in the cultural offices, Yevtushenko was haunted by a growing suspicion that the dogmatists' defensive position was only tactical. Influenced by these sentiments, he had already (the previous fall) written the poem "The Heirs of Stalin." In this poem he pathetically warned against the intrigues of the neo-Stalinists which he, perhaps mostly for the political effect, linked with the anti-Soviet attitude of the Albanian leader Enver Hoxha and through this directly with Maoism which could then not be openly criticized. Yevtushenko had at this time Khrushchev's ear. The Party chairman had some human qualities—he could for example appreciate open opposition if he only felt that it was not directed against him personally and was dictated by concern for "the cause." This unique trait was demonstrated in the grotesque clash at the Manege with the sculptor Ernst Neizvestny a few weeks later. Khrushchev obviously liked the "non-Party member" Yevtushenko for his careless charm, his popularity among the Soviet youth and the talent to win sympathy from radical intellectuals in the West. As long as it was possible, he even defended Yevtushenko's behavior and frank statements during the latter's tour of West Germany and France even though he later had to curb his flow of praises when Yevtushenko published his even more candid "memoirs" in France. Yevtushenko was the only famous Soviet poet who was permitted to attend the macabre ceremony when soldiers from the Kursk and Riazan garrisons, towards the end of the 22nd Party Congress, removed Joseph Stalin's embalmed corpse from the Mausoleum at Red Square—the highlight of the de-Stalinization campaign.

Now, when the dispute over Solzhenitsyn was over, Khrushchev did not hesitate to act. He ordered the Party daily, *Pravda,* to publish Yevtushenko's poem. This happened on October 21. The spotlight suddenly and clearly turned on Yevtushenko. The same day, a Sunday, another of Yevtushenko's controversial anti-Stalinist poems, "Fear is Dying in Russia", was printed in the most popular daily in Moscow, the *Komsomolskaya Pravda,* a publication of the Young Communist League (Komsomol). The situation was utterly confused. The signal for a hardening of the anti-Stalinist line was given by a poet who was not a Party member, and who some years previously, had been expelled from the Young Communist League and from the writers' college—The Gorky Institute.

Precisely a month later, attention was focused on a piece by an unknown former political prisoner, a "zek". Once more a non-Party member, and even worse, a man who had been punished for political crimes, was allowed to tell the bitter facts about the atrocities during Stalin's era over the heads of the almighty censorship agency, Glavlit, and the Secret Police. On December 20, 1962 the 11th issue of *Novy Mir* carrying the story of the prison-camp inmate, Ivan Denisovich Shukov, was distributed. The copies in the bookstores in Moscow and Leningrad were all sold out in a few hours. Besides its artistic qualities the story was a great cultural and political event for a number of reasons.

Nikita Khrushchev had personally intervened to get it published. The story was therefore regarded as a kind of "Party Document." Also, it was the first officially sanctioned description of life in Stalin's labor camps. It gave substance to the kind of revealing literature (such as Kravchenko's *I Chose Freedom*) that had been published in the West but was regarded as "anti-Soviet," deceitful and slanderous, in the Soviet Union.

It was the first officially-backed writing by a rehabilitated man who was not a Party member.

The writer had been rehabilitated after internment for something that was considered a crime at the time it occurred. The Slovakian writer Pavel Licko maintains that Solzhenitsyn refused to plead innocent before the rehabilitation tribunal. He had in fact criticized Stalin in his letters from the front (to a friend) during the period 1944–45, and in prose sketches which he was carrying in his map folder when he was arrested. Worried members of the Party asked themselves whether Khrushchev's intervention in favor of Solzhenitsyn could be seen as a sanction of the right to maintain an opposite point of view within, as well as without, the Party framework, or was it, to put it straight, calculated to undermine the principles of "the democratic centralism", and "the leading role", of the Party?

The story was the very first totally uncensored work of a high literary standard with a controversial content critical of the society.

Two days after the distribution of the magazine had started in Moscow, Nikita Khrushchev told a plenary session of the Central Committee that he had "recommended" Glavlit (the censorship agency) to approve publication of *One Day in the Life of Ivan Denisovich*. At the same time he disclosed that members of the Presidium had been opposed to the publication. He said that he had explained to them that "nobody has the right to change the writer's version." This statement gave birth to rumors that Khrushchev planned to abolish censorship for literature.

Khrushchev's speech, with the indications of freedom and the disqualification of the censors, marked a turning point. His opponents now took up the offensive and after the so-called Manège incident at the end of December, it became obvious that Khrushchev could not stand up against a united Establishment which was supported by leading politicians who had been outvoted, for instance, in the Solzhenitsyn affair. Because of the Manège coup the dogmatists in the Party apparatus and the Artists' Union were able to force Khrushchev to take position against the new trends of the old generation. The party leader had thereby dropped one shoe. The surprisingly long series of meetings between the politicians and the cultural elite that followed in the succeeding months gradually came to deal less with the question of nonconformist painting and more with Khrushchev's de-Stalinization line and politics in general. The struggle became more openly dramatic and found outlets in the form of lists with names for and against, open letters and appeals from, among others, Ehrenburg and other "liberals" of the twenties. Khrushchev was forced to retreat where he obviously had planned an offensive, and the position of the censorship was again strengthened remarkably. Khrushchev himself was even forced into a partial rehabilitation of Stalin in a speech which was published in the press on March 9, 1963, four days after the 10th anniversary of the dictator's death.

The dogmatists, the conformists and the "neo-Stalinists" quickly gained control of the debate which centered around the invisible but omnipresent Aleksandr Solzhenitsyn. At these meetings several of the most prominent young writers and artists, including Yevtushenko, Voznesensky, Rozhdestvensky and Neizvestny, were forced to make apologies.

Solzhenitsyn, however, refused from the very beginning to compromise. The more Khrushchev halted and retreated in order to regain at least some of his political prestige, the more controversial and dangerous (for his regime) became the literary work he had personally intervened to save. The Party leader never publicly retracted his arguments favorable to the new writer, but it soon became obvious that Solzhenitsyn would no longer be enjoying any privileges of freedom from censorship. The three prose works by Solzhenitsyn which were published in *Novy Mir* in the following months—*Matryona's House, An Incident at Krechetovka Station* and *For the Good of the Cause* had been approved by Glavlit, probably without modifications, earlier when Solzhenitsyn was still regarded as a protégé of Khrushchev. But the more the criticism against Solzhenitsyn was stepped up, the harder became Glavlit's attitude to him. Eventually, it was openly demonstrated that not even Solzhenitsyn was above censorship. The production of the play, *The Love-Girl and the Innocent,* which had been accepted by the Artistic Council of the Sovremennik Theater at the end of 1962 was now postponed. The scheduled publication of several of Solzhenitsyn's short stories was halted. Since Khrushchev's fall only an article on the Russian language and a short story: *Zachar-Kalita,* by Solzhenitsyn have been published in the Soviet Union.

Childhood and Youth

Alexander Isaevich Solzhenitsyn was born on December 11, 1918, at Kislovodsk ("Sour Water"), a northern Caucasian resort which, in those days, had a population of some 20,000. Kislovodsk was famous for its wonderful, sheltered climate, its mineral water (Narzán) and its wild, treeless mountains which Lermontov lovingly described in *A Hero of Our Times*.

Solzhenitsyn's father, Isai, had been a student of linguistics at the University of Moscow. He never finished his studies. The outbreak of World War I on August 1, 1914, put an end to his academic career. He enlisted, received crash training in an artillery school (as did his son 27 years later) and served (so did his son later) during practically the whole World War as an officer with fighting units on the Russian-German frontline. In 1917, the year of the Revolution, he married Taisiya Zakharovna Shcherbak.

In the summer of 1918, six months before Aleksandr was born, Isai Solzhenitsyn was killed in a hunting accident. Aleksandr grew up in extremely poor circumstances during the chaos of the Revolution and the Civil War. The mother, who refused to remarry despite Alexandr's wish for her to do so, did a poorly-paid office job and barely managed to support herself and her son.

In 1924, the year Lenin died, Aleksandr and his mother moved to the big industrial center of Rostov-na-Donu (Rostov-on-Don) where she was employed as a typist and stenographer.

The city was then the center of the Don Cossacks. It had been controlled back and forth by "The Whites" and "The Reds" until 1920 when the legendary Semen Budenny's "Red Cavalry" conquered the city. This region was the scene of the

15

violent events told by Isaak Babel in *Konarimya* (*Red Cavalry*) and by Mikhail Sholokhov in *And Quiet Flows the Don.*

Rostov, situated not far from the Sea of Azov, had at this time almost a quarter of a million inhabitants. It was an important industrial city with tobacco and leather factories, paper mills, a harbor and a cultural center. The Federal Don University had Faculties for Medicine, Pedagogy, Social Science and "Fizmat" (Physics and Mathematics). The Don Museum gave a good indication of the comparatively liberal cultural policies of that period. Represented there were works of the great masters of the past as well as works following the very latest Movements: Futurism, Cubism, neo-Academicism.

The city was growing quickly and had, shortly before the beginning of the second World War, a population of more than half a million.

Solzhenitsyn's works, however, carry very few references to the events of this period.

Solzhenitsyn has mentioned the fact that his mother lived in utter loneliness and isolation and had to cope with illness during the years they were in Rostov-na-Donu. They were poor and lived in circumstances close to misery. His concern for her (and also, economic reasons) made Solzhenitsyn remain in Rostov-na-Donu through the years preceding the war.

His mother died of tuberculosis during the war (in 1944). A serious-minded, extremely gifted and independent child, he became aware quite early, of the tragic political drama that had started to unfold in the nation. Through Gleb Nerzhin, in many aspects his *alter ego,* Solzhenitsyn describes in *The First Circle* his own awakening:

In that same way, through some strange inward sense, Nerzhin had, since adolescence, been hearing a mute bell—all the groans, cries, shouts of the dying, carried by a steady, insistent wind away from human ears. He grew up without reading a single book by Mayne Reid but at the age of twelve he had gone through an enormous pile of Izvestia as tall as he was and he had read about the trial of the saboteur engineers. From the very first, the boy did not believe what he read. He did not know why—his reason could not grasp it—but he could clearly see that it was all a lie. He knew engineers in his friends' families, and he could not imagine them committing sabotage.

At thirteen and fourteen Gleb did not run out to play in the street when he had finished studying, but sat reading the newspapers. He knew the Party leaders by name, their positions, the Soviet military leaders, the Soviet ambassadors in every country, and the foreign ambassadors in the Soviet Union. He read all the speeches made at the congresses, and the memoirs of the Old Bolsheviks, and the shifting history of the Party—there had been several versions and each was different. In school, too, in the fourth grade, he had already been introduced to the elements of political economy, and from the fifth grade on he had Social Sciences almost every day. He was given *In Memory of Herzen* to read, and again and again he pored over the Lenin volume.

Either because his ear was young or because he read more than there was in the newspapers, he clearly sensed the falsity in the exaggerated, stifling exaltation of one man, always one man! If he was everything, did it not mean that other men were nothing? Out of pure protest Gleb refused to let himself be carried away.

Gleb was only a ninth-grader on the December morning when he looked into a display window where a newspaper was posted and read that Kirov had been killed. And suddenly, like a blinding light, it became clear to him that Stalin and no one else had killed Kirov. Because he was the only one who would profit by his death! A feeling of aching loneliness seized him—the grown men, crowded near him, did not understand that simple truth.

Then the same Old Bolsheviks, who had made the entire Revolution and whose whole life it had been, began by the dozens and the hundreds to drift into non-existence. Some, not waiting to be arrested, swallowed poison in their apartments; others hanged themselves in their houses outside the city. But most let themselves be arrested. They appeared in court and unaccountably confessed, loudly condemned themselves with the worst vilifications, and admitted serving in all foreign intelligence agencies in the world. It was so overdone, so crude, so excessive, that only a stone ear could fail to hear the lie.

Did people really not hear? Russian writers who dared trace their spiritual inheritance from Pushkin and Tolstoy wrote sickly-sweet eulogies of the tyrant. Russian composers, trained in the Herzen Street conservatory, laid their servile hymns at his pedestal.

For Gleb Nerzhin the mute bell thundered through his entire youth. An inviolable decision took root in him: to learn and understand! Strolling the boulevards of his native city when it would have been more fitting to sigh over a girl, Gleb went around dreaming of the day he would sort everything out and would, perhaps, even penetrate within the walls where those people, as one, had vilified themselves before they died. Perhaps inside those walls it could be understood.

In 1936 Aleksandr Solzhenitsyn graduated from the intermediate school in Rostov-na-Donu with brilliant marks in Russian and Science.

He had already for a long time dreamt of being a writer and had even sent his first literary efforts to different cultural magazines including one that was edited by Konstantin Fedin, but he was turned down everywhere.

He was also forced to give up all plans to get a suitable literary education. There was no such program available at the University of Rostov. The concern for his mother and lack of economic means made it impossible for him to get his education somewhere else, for example in Moscow.

In school he showed an obvious talent for Mathematics and Physics. So when in 1937, the year of terror, he was forced to give up his plans to be a writer, he sent his application to the Faculty of Mathematics and Physics at the Don University.

In spite of the fact that he regarded his studies of "Fizmat" as a necessity of life only, he was very successful and was awarded one of the important scholarships named after Stalin.

But he was of a complicated character. In 1939 he decided, despite all difficulties, to educate himself as a writer. He therefore attended a two-year course in Literature at MIIFLI, the Institute of History, Philosophy and Literature in Moscow, while pursuing, at the same time, his studies in Science. He completed his education towards the end of 1940. This intensive period of studies is described in *The First Circle*:

There was no old Russia, but the Soviet Union instead. In it there was a great city. Young Gleb had grown up in that city. From the cornucopia of science, success showered upon him. He found out that his mind worked quickly but that there were others whose minds worked even faster, whose wealth of knowledge oppressed him. The People remained on the bookshelves. He was convinced that the only people who matter are those who carry in their heads the accumulated culture of the world: encyclopedists, connoisseurs of antiquity, men who value beauty—highly educated, manysided men and multi-faceted leaders. One must belong to that elite! The lot of those who fail is distress.

At the beginning of June 1941, only a few days prior to the German attack on the Soviet Union, Aleksandr Solzhenitsyn graduated from the University of Rostov as a licentiate in Mathematics and Physics.

But at this time he had also become intensively interested in another form of art. At the end of the thirties the famous theater director Yuri Zavadsky, a favorite student of Vakhtangov, had been deported from Moscow to Rostov-na-Donu, where he organized a theatrical school.

Solzhenitsyn visited this school during his free time. Zavadsky later said that he regarded Solzhenitsyn as a very talented comedian. Solzhenitsyn's physician however put an end to this theatrical adventure. He was suffering from a chronic inflammation of the larynx. In spite of this, he never lost his affection for the theater—his works are full of references to the theater, and he has written several plays of varying quality such as: *Feast of the Conquerors* (which he created "in his mind" in the concentration camp at Ekibastuz and which was later to be used as a weapon in the campaign against him), *The Love-Girl and the Innocent* (which was accepted by the Sovremennik Theater in Moscow at the end of 1962, but was later banned) and *The Light That Is in You.*

An incident in *One Day in the Life of Ivan Denisovich* is very characteristic. Some prisoners queuing up for food in the camp were discussing a play created by Yuri Zavadsky, after reading a review of it in the evening newspaper *Vechernaya Moskva.*

The critic Yuri Karyakin, one of the most eager defenders of Solzhenitsyn's work, had pointed out that Zavadsky, in December of 1950, a few weeks before the incident took place, was actually the first to produce an ideologically challenging play, *Dawn over Moscow,* by Surov. Zavadsky's production had received a positive review, as challenging as the play itself, in the *Vechernaya Moskva,* which stressed "the actual truthfulness" of the play. This illustrates to what extent Solzhenitsyn works with factual material, even in the details.

Solzhenitsyn later confided in his friends, (and the Slovakian writer, Pavel Licko, also mentions it) that this restless and confused period preceding the war was the luckiest in his whole life. He was then not aware of the cancer, and thus filled with great energy, he was successful in his studies.

In 1940 he married Natalya Alexeyevna Reshetovskaya, the sweetheart of his youth, who is the model for Nadya in *The First Circle.*

Nadya and Gleb had lived together for one year, a year of running around carrying bulging briefcases. Both were fifth-year students, writing term papers and taking state examinations.

Natalya Reshetovskaya was also a licentiate, but with Physical Chemistry, and later, Biochemistry as specialties. During their early marriage she was a teacher at the Agricultural Institute of Rostov-na-Donu.

Solzhenitsyn was drafted on October 18, 1941. It was to take a decade and a half before he saw his wife again.

Solzhenitsyn's War

In the New Year of 1945 Stalin's *stavka* (headquarters) were touching up their plan of the Köningsberg attack, which was part of the large-scale offensive against East Prussia.

This offensive was launched on January 13 by the Third Belorussian Army Corps. The following day forces from the Second Corps were also sent into action.

Breaking through the German defense lines, however, was harder than expected. The atmosphere at the headquarters grew more irritating and so also the pressure on the military and political front leaders.

According to the official Soviet view of history as reflected in, among other publications, *The Great Patriotic War of the Soviet Union* published by the Ministry of Defense in 1967, the main reason for the delay was that the offensive did not include any moments of surprise whatsoever for the Germans and that the weather conditions were exceptionally unfavorable:

"During the first days of the offensive a heavy fog covered the battlefield. It did not only hinder the use of airplanes but also, to a large extent, made the observation of the progress of the battle very difficult since visibility did not exceed 150–200 meters (50–66 feet). This consequently decreased the effectiveness of the artillery fire and restrained the military leadership."

The difficulties continued even after the break-through on January 18. The German resistance grew stronger. The Soviet military leaders were displeased with the slow progress of the operation. Nervousness pervaded all levels of the general staff, especially the artillery forces where the effectiveness was reduced considerably because of the persistent fog.

This was "fatal ground" in Russian war history. On the mili-

21

tary maps of the same region the Czar's headquarters thirty one years ago had charted the course of what was to become Russia's most disastrous and humiliating defeat in the first World War—the Samsonov catastrophe—in which the second Russian Army was destroyed and the betrayed commander, General Aleksandr Samsonov, shot himself.

Aleksandr Solzhenitsyn knew these sites and the details of the catastrophe better than any other officer in this sector of the front. Already, during his last year in the Gymnasium at Rostov-na-Donu in 1936 he had started to gather information about the collapse of the Second Army. Now he was able to see for himself these same places under similar circumstances during the war. Solzhenitsyn intermittently worked on this material on which was based the novel *August, 1914,* which he completed only in October–November 1970.

One of the military officers who worked under great pressure from the high command was Major General Travkin, who commanded the division to which Aleksandr Solzhenitsyn's battery belonged. This general, according to the Slovakian writer Pavel Licko, was Solzhenitsyn's true friend and was to play an important part in Solzhenitsyn's life.

At the time of the Köningsberg offensive Aleksandr Solzhenitsyn had just turned twenty-six, but his military career was remarkable.

When the war broke out, he had just left the university and was teaching Physics and Mathematics. He had chosen teaching without enthusiasm and regarded it only as a means of earning a living, for he was still undecided between this profession and his dreams of being a writer. The German attack on the Soviet Union on June 22 solved his dilemma. He was drafted on October 18 and was first picked out to serve as a driver on transport wagons, for his health was not satisfactory. Solzhenitsyn has told Pavel Licko that his first companions in arms were "old, sick Cossacks" and that he was in charge of about one hundred horses.

In the story of Gleb Nerzhin in *The First Circle* Solzhenitsyn

gives an account of his own wartime experience in the winter
of 1941–42:

"But the war began, and Nerzhin was first sent out as a
driver on transport wagons. Clumsy, choking with shame, he
rounded up horses in the pasture, bridled them, jumped on
their backs. He did not know how to ride or to harness a horse,
how to pitch hay, and every nail he hit invariably bent as if
to mock the inept workman. And the more bitter Nerzhin's lot,
the louder the laughter of the unshaven, profane, pitiless and
extremely disagreeable people around him.
    Then Nerzhin worked up to the rank of artillery officer. He
became young and capable again. He walked around wearing
a tight belt and elegantly waving a broken cane, because he
had no other weapon. He rode recklessly on the running boards
of speeding trucks, cursed heatedly, and was ready to attack
at midnight or in the rain and he led the obedient, loyal, indus-
trious, and, consequently, pleasant people. And they, his own
small personal people, listened agreeably to his propaganda
talks about the Big People who had risen as one man."

During the first months of catastrophic defeats nobody
listened to the driver's request to be transferred to the artillery,
where he could make better use of his scientific knowledge and
talent. He served in the transport service until the spring of
1942. Finally, he was saved by an officer in the division. This
officer had more or less by chance discovered Solzhenitsyn's
mathematical talent and managed to obtain a transfer for him.
Solzhenitsyn is said to have called this incident "the first
mathematical rescue". Mathematics would in fact, come to his
rescue in even more difficult situations.
    In the spring of 1942 Aleksandr Solzhenitsyn was entered
for a year-long, concentrated course at an artillery school and
toward the end of the year he moved to Gorky, "the Detroit
of the Soviet Union." He narrates his experiences during the
two-week trip there in *An Incident At Krechetovka Station.*
    He was appointed Second Lieutenant the same year and
served as commander of the listening post of a reconnaissance

battery on the advanced frontline. He advanced quickly to the
rank of Lieutenant, then First Lieutenant and finally to that of
Captain and Battery Commander, participating in the defense
of Leningrad as well as in the historically famous armored
battle of Kursk-Oryol, and the offensives in East Prussia. In
The First Circle, he describes these places thus:

> Between that world and the world of today there had been
> the forests below Lake Ilmen, the hills and ravines of Oryol, the
> sands and marshes of Belorussia, the fat Polish farms, the tile
> roofs of German cities.

One of his comrades in arms, Captain Melnikov, and other
anonymous officers, later testified before the Rehabilitation
Commission that Solzhenitsyn had "fought with bravery for the
Fatherland, on several occasions had shown heroic courage and,
in combat, had inspired the soldiers in the unit he led.
Solzhenitsyn's Battery showed the best discipline and morale
in the whole division".

These were qualities his superiors in the Army had sensed
and appreciated. There are no indications whatsoever that he
was regarded as a controversial officer. At the time of the
Köningsberg offensive he has been honored with two decorations
for bravery: the Order of the Patriotic War and the Order of
the Red Star. They were, indeed, not worthless medals.

At the beginning of February, during the battle of Königs-
berg, Captain Aleksandr Solzhenitsyn was suddenly called to
Major General Travkin, commander of the division.

In General Travkin's office were two men, whom Solzhenitsyn, only after a while, could identify as members of
the NKVD's counter-espionage section SMERSH: (*Smerch
Shpionam,* Death for the spies).

Without realizing the meaning of the present situation he
noticed that General Travkin was remarkably nervous and
tense.

Despite the risks Travkin was taking by showing a "traitor"
sympathy and by treating him according to the traditional military code, the General was most anxious to follow the military

etiquette. So he ordered the 26-year-old captain to hand over his service weapon, a pistol.

After this short ceremony the SMERSH agents jumped on Solzhenitsyn and tore off his stripes and distinctions.

He was arrested.

In this humiliating situation something happened that forever remained indelible in Solzhenitsyn's memory and which he mentioned to Pavel Licko as one of the most courageous actions he witnessed during the entire war. General Travkin grasped the hand of the arrested "traitor" to demonstrate his friendship and sympathy. Thereafter, Solzhenitsyn was taken away.

The arrest took place in early February of 1945. The exact date has not been established—it is not even mentioned in the rehabilitation protocol.

The Imprisonment

The Lubyanka Prison

Then Nerzhin was arrested. During his very first interrogation, in his first transit prison, in his first camp, struck dumb by these deadly blows, he had been horrified by his perception of the other side of certain members of the "elite": in circumstances where firmness of character, strength of will, and loyalty to one's friends were vital to a prisoner and could determine the fate of his comrades, these delicate, sensitive, highly educated persons who valued beauty often turned out to be cowards, quick to cave in, adroit in excusing their own vileness. They soon degenerated into traitors, beggars and hypocrites. (*The First Circle*)

"I was arrested for my naive conceptions. I was not ignorant about the fact that we were forbidden to write about military information in the letters from the front, but I thought we were allowed to think and ponder."

This remark was made by Aleksandr Solzhenitsyn in an interview with Pavel Licko. Solzhenitsyn had "for a long time maintained a critical attitude toward Stalin", and this criticism was certainly radical. Stalin had "betrayed the Leninist cause", was "responsible for the catastrophies of the First War period and spoke a language full of grammatical slips". This information is probably correct, even if there are reasons for skepticism regarding Licko's statements. The Slovakian writer was one of the shadowy figures of the so-called "Prague Spring". In Bratislava he was almost regarded as a *provocateur,* who had worked as a Soviet agent during the World War.

The rehabilitation protocol of February 6, 1956, states that

Aleksandr Solzhenitsyn was arrested because of the contents of "a diary" and of letters to a comrade at the front, N. D. Vitkevich.

But this was not the whole truth. Solzhenitsyn has told his friends that he was arrested as a result of letters he had written in 1944–45 to a childhood friend and schoolmate, Vitkevich, and for documents that were found by SMERSH in a map folder when he was arrested. These documents were "outlines for stories" and "certain reflections" (which probably could be regarded as diary notes).

From the Köningsberg front Aleksandr Solzhenitsyn was taken to NKVD's transit prison for political prisoners—Lubyanka—in Moscow. The humiliating routine before admittance which aimed at breaking the prisoner, physically as well as psychologically, is described in detail in the chapter on the arrest of Innokenty Volodin in *The First Circle*.

After more than four months of interrogation, on July 7, 1945, Solzhenitsyn was sentenced, in his absence, to eight years in the ITL (correction camp). He was sentenced after an entirely administrative procedure by a so-called "troika" or OSO (Osoboye Soveshchaniye), a special NKVD tribunal.

The evidence included the confiscated letters to Vitkevich, Solzhenitsyn's "reflections" and the prose sketches in the map folder, reports by informers and protocols from alleged or actual hearings with persons in his surrounding. The sentence was based on the penal code of the RSFSR (Russian Soviet Federated Socialist Republic), sections 58:10, part 2 and 58:11.

Section 58 of the penal code deals with "counter revolutionary crimes", while section 58:10 concerns propaganda and agitation calling for the overthrow, undermining or weakening of the Soviet regime as well as the distribution, preparation or possession of literature with the same purpose.

Section 58:11 anticipates all kinds of organized activities, aimed at preparing and committing this kind of crime as well as membership of an organization formed to plan and commit any of these crimes.

If the crime is committed during times of "mass unrest" or

in wartime it is considered "an aggravating circumstance" and the maximum sentence is "death before the firing squad or the declaration of the accused as an enemy of the working masses" in addition to confiscation of property and loss of Soviet citizenship.

But according to the rehabilitation protocol the indictment did not only deal with the content of Solzhenitsyn's map folder and the letters to Vitkevich. Solzhenitsyn was also accused of "having carried on anti-Soviet agitation among his friends and taken action for the formation of an anti-Soviet organization from 1940 to the time of his arrest in February of 1945".

The rehabilitation document shows that the friends who allegedly had been exposed to this anti-Soviet agitation were two unidentified persons by the names Simonyan and Simonyants and a certain Reshetovskaya, evidently identical with Solzhenitsyn's first wife, Natalya.

Aleksandr Solzhenitsyn allegedly told Pavel Licko that he never considered himself guilty of the crimes he was accused of. He had, however, in fact criticized Stalin as an ideologist, military leader and "stylist".

Through other sources we know that Solzhenitsyn in his letters to Vitkevich continued earlier discussions with his friend on the subject mentioned by Licko. In these letters, however, Stalin was never mentioned by name but was called, as was the practice of that time, Khoziayin, The Boss.

As early as 1944—probably even earlier, and perhaps when still a child—Solzhenitsyn's attitude to Stalin was similar to the attitude Nikita Khrushchev was to adopt as late as the mid-fifties. Solzhenitsyn's criticism of Stalin as a military leader during the first catastrophic period of the war was completely in line with controversial historian Aleksandr Nekrich's opinion which, judging from his several works on war history, was, at least for some time, shared by military leaders, and even by Marshals surrounding Khrushchev. At the beginning of the sixties, this opinion of Stalin had in fact become so common that it was reflected in several literary works, among them Grigori Baklanov's *July, 41*, Konstantin Simonov's *The Living and the Dead,* and Yuri Bondaryev's *Silence.* Aleksandr Solzhenitsyn has elaborated on this criticism against Stalin in *The First Circle.*

Even concerning Stalin's betrayal of the Leninist cause, the ideologists of the Khrushchev regime followed the same line as Solzhenitsyn, even if they never carried it as far as he did. This view of Stalin as a distorter of ideology totally dominated fiction literature, memoirs and historical drama from the early sixties to the middle of that decade. The disclosure of this ideological "treason" was probably the most central theme of Solzhenitsyn's works in the sixties. This criticism is particularly painstaking in *The First Circle* and *Cancer Ward.* Almost everything else he has written demonstrates in different ways the tragic consequences of the Stalinist "treason" against the Leninist cause.

The criticism against Stalin as an authority on Linguistics and as a "stylist", which is not mentioned in the rehabilitation protocol, is probably apprehended correctly by Pavel Licko. Proof of Licko's opinion of Solzhenitsyn's attitude to linguistic matters can be found in several passages of *The First Circle* and also in an article published in *Literaturnaya Gazetta,* on November 4, 1965.

In a protest letter that Lidya Chukovskaya—Kornei Chukovsky's adopted daughter—wrote to *Literaturnaya Gazetta* in 1968, but which was never published in the Soviet Union, she confirms some of the statements Pavel Licko attributed to Solzhenitsyn. She writes in one passage:

"Ever since his youth (earlier than others) he had seen through Stalin. Later, as a writer, he began to unmask Stalinism—and not only in his diaries and letters. This is the reason for the persecutions against him in the past and his tragic situation today".

The NKVD troika sentenced Aleksandr Solzhenitsyn to eight years in the ITL (correction camp). After months in the transit prison, Lubyanka, he was transferred to the Butyrki prison in Moscow.

The Butyrki Prison

In the cell at "Butyrka", which he describes in detail in the chapter entitled "Buddha's Smile" in *The First Circle,* were some seventy men, mainly intellectual political prisoners, among whom was Nikolai Vladimirovich Timofeyev-Resovsky, the geneticist and radiobiologist, who was arrested after a conflict with "the scientific dictator" Trofim Lysenko, Stalin's special protégé. Zhorez Medvedev, one of Aleksandr Solzhenitsyn's closest friends, says in a book he wrote about the official policy toward science, that the geneticist organized a "technical-scientific society" in this cell. The members gathered daily at the window, after their bread rations had been handed out, to listen to different lectures. On one occasion, according to Medvedev's book titled *The Medvedev Papers: The Plight of Soviet Science* which was smuggled out to the West, Solzhenitsyn lectured on atomic energy.

Only six of the society's seventeen members were still living in 1970. These were Timofeyev-Resovsky, Solzhenitsyn, the physicist V. Kogan, the specialists on energy: N. A. Semenov and S. S. Karpov and the chemist Martur.

Solzhenitsyn was transferred from Butyrki to a "mixed type" correction camp (as it is called), which is an institution where violent criminals as well as political prisoners are locked up. This camp was identical to the one described in Solzhenitsyn's play, *The Love-Girl and the Innocent.*

The Kaluga Gates: A Construction Site

For some time one of Solzhenitsyn's jobs was to lay parquet floors at a construction site on the present Leninsky Prospekt in Moscow. He described it to Pavel Licko as "a big building with an ornamental portal and a store called Spartak on the first floor". The building was reserved for NKVD officials and their families. This period is also captured in *The First Circle:* "At the Kaluga Gates, is the MVD apartment house, the rounded one with the tower. Our camp was building it in 1945, and I was working as an apprentice, laying parquet floors. And I learned today that Roitman is living in that very apartment house. So I've been worrying ever since about my workmanship or, if you prefer, my prestige. Do my floors squeak or don't they? After all, if they squeak, that means it was jerry-built flooring. And here I am, unable to correct it!"

According to rather widely-spread information in the Soviet Union, which was later reported by the foreign press, this NKVD building which is close to the Neskuchny Garden, was later given to the Soviet Academy of Sciences. A great number of academicians are still living there. In the sixties, after Solzhenitsyn had become a famous writer, he was once invited by a scientist who lived in one of "his" apartments. Solzhenitsyn then had the pleasure of discovering that he had not done a bad job. It was the only apartment in the whole house without squeaking floors.

GULAG, the Prison Administration of the Ministry of State Security, was, in a grotesque manner, operated along business lines. In this "commercially" run state office which, among other things, had built several famous canals, railroads and power stations, certain "efficiency reforms" were being carried out during Stalin's time. So Aleksandr Solzhenitsyn had to fill in a form giving his background. Thanks to this document a security official discovered his knowledge of Mathematics and Physics.

Mavrino

This was his "second mathematical rescue". In 1946 he was taken to a special prison outside Moscow, a so-called "sharashka", a scientific research institute under the aegis of the MVD and the MGB. With the exception of the supervising and administrative personnel, the prison was run entirely by political prisoners, all of them intellectuals and some of them outstanding scientists. In the Mavrino Prison (as it is called in *The First Circle*) with its relatively endurable labor conditions and adequate food rations, Aleksandr Solzhenitsyn worked as a mathematician for about four years, that is, for half his prison term:

The sharashka took its name from the nearby village of Mavrino, which had long been absorbed into the Moscow city limits. The sharashka had been established on a July evening a little more than three years ago. Some fifteen zeks had been brought in from concentration camps and delivered to an old manor house in the Moscow suburb, encircled, for the occasion, by barbed wire. At the sharashka those early days were now referred to as the "Krylov" period and were remembered as a pastoral era. At that time one could walk freely at evening in what had since become the forbidden "zone", lie on the dewy grass which, against all prison regulations, had not been cut . . . .

No one in the sharashka at that time knew what its field scientific endeavor would be. They were kept busy unpacking a vast number of crates delivered by two freight trains . . . rounding up comfortable chairs and desks . . . sorting out-of-date and broken equipment for telephone, ultra high-frequency radio communication, and acoustics. It turned out that the best apparatus and the papers documenting the newest scientific research had been stolen or destroyed by the Germans . . . .

Since then the grass had been cut. The gates to the yard where the zeks had their exercise were open only at the ringing of a bell. The sharashka had passed from Beria's jurisdiction to Abakumov's and had been put to work on secret telephone communications. The assignment was to have taken one year, but it had already stretched to two, becoming larger, confused, and encompassing more and more related projects. And here, on Rubin's and Nerzhin's desks, it had reached the stage of identifying voices on the telephone, and discovering what makes a human voice unique.

One of Solzhenitsyn's fellow prisoners in the Mavrino sharashka was Lev Kopelev, a writer and philologist of the German language and literature. He had also been arrested in East Prussian towards the end of the war. Kopelev has served as the prototype for Lev Rubin in *The First Circle*.

The inmates of the sharashka produced, among other things, advanced T.V. sets. They were also developing electronic methods to identify and decipher voices. These methods were as important for the eavesdropping by the Security Police as for the confidential telephone conversations of the political leaders.

"I lived there in good circumstances", Solzhenitsyn later told Pavel Licko. "It is true that there were bars across the windows and our freedom to move around was limited to a few minutes' walk in the prison yard, but we had the right to eat and I had my work to do."

Ekibastuz

After a year at the "sharashka" Solzhenitsyn was sent to "the lowest circle": a labor camp exclusively for political prisoners in the town of Ekibastuz between Pavlodar and Tselinograd in northeast Kazakhstan, "an island in the GULAG archipelago." It was an enormous, complex camp of the size of France, out in the Central Asian semidesert. This notorious camp conglomerate is known as Karlag and is the scene for the events told in *One Day in the Life of Ivan Denisovich*. All the events occurred during one single day in January 1951. Like Ivan Denisovich Shukhov, Aleksandr Solzhenitsyn had to wear labels with his number on the chest, the back and on one knee. In this camp Solzhenitsyn worked from time to time in an intolerable climate as a bricklayer, founder and construction worker.

After about three years in this Central Asian inferno he was released in February 1953. However, he still had to spend a few more weeks under surveillance in a transit camp on his way to Kok-Terek in Kazakhstan where he was going to be deported. The deportation, which had been announced without formal court decision was described in the official protocol as "eternal" (which meant that he had no chance of pardon or of ever getting out).

But by a strange coincidence he was suddenly given back his freedom on March 5, 1953. "An old, deaf woman woke me up early that morning begging me to go down into the street to listen to the news that was roaring out of the loudspeakers. So I walked out. It was the announcement of Stalin's death."

This was how Solzhenitsyn described his release to Pavel Licko.

Kok-Terek

Solzhenitsyn settled down in the Uzbek village of Kok-Terek ("The green poplar"), southwest of the lake of Balkhash in the Dzhambul District. He tells us in the essay, *The Right Hand,* that he had to report in person to the local NKVD authorities every second week.

Living in a mud hut and teaching the Uzbek village children Mathematics and Physics, Solzhenitsyn started writing seriously.

Already, in the camp at Ekibastuz he had undergone surgery. The physicians had diagnosed cancer and had removed a sizable tumor. The diagnosis, however, was not disclosed to him.

The operation failed. After some time at Kok-Terek the pain grew worse and eventually unendurable. The village had no competent physician and Solzhenitsyn was forbidden to leave the place. Toward the end of 1953 he was dying. He was unable to eat or sleep. He was being "poisoned by cancer".

Tashkent: The Cancer Clinic

Solzhenitsyn writes in *The Right Hand* that the local NKVD commandant of Kok-Terek hesitated for a long time before he finally gave him permission to go to Tashkent, the capital of Uzbekistan.

He was barely alive when he reached the cancer clinic there. The doctors gave him no hope. Thanks to radium therapy, however, they managed to save his life. His experience of the illness and the treatment in Tashkent in 1954 is the source of *The Right Hand* as well as the great novel *Cancer Ward.*

Kok-Terek

After the stay in the cancer clinic in Tashkent, Solzhenitsyn returned to his "eternal" deportation at Kok-Terek where he continued to teach Mathematics and Physics while carrying on his secret literary work. In this small Uzbek village he completed the play, *The Love-Girl and the Innocent,* and started writing *The First Circle.*

In connection with the 20th Party Congress in 1956 when Nikita Khrushchev made his famous "secret" speech about the Stalinist atrocities, the "eternal" deportation of Aleksandr Solzhenitsyn was annulled. His case was resumed on February 6 and the earlier sentence reversed. In June 1956, he left his place of exile.

Freedom

He was permitted to return to the European part of Russia—a dream he had never dared to hope would come true. He settled down in the district of Vladimir, where he completed his story *Matryona's House*. After a short time in Vladimir he moved to Riazan.

Riazan is an old, genuine Russian town that goes back to the 11th century. It is situated on the banks of the river Oka, about 280 miles from Moscow. In the mid-fifties it had a population of about 100,000. The city has several colleges and a prosperous machinery, timber and textile industry.

When his deportation was repealed he came into contact again with his wife, Natalya Reshetovskaya, who, while he was in prison, had remarried and had two children. Solzhenitsyn apparently regarded the divorce as final. In *The Right Hand,* the events of which occurred in 1954, he pictures himself as totally lonesome without any close relatives.

Solzhenitsyn's family relations after his release are uncertain. In 1956, Natalya Reshetovskaya, who in both her marriages had retained her maiden name—a very common practice in the Soviet Union—obviously left her second husband. She was reunited with Solzhenitsyn at Riazan, where he was teaching Physics and Mathematics at the intermediate level. His wife was employed as a lecturer in Chemistry at the Agricultural Institute of Riazan.

After years of prison and deportation Aleksandr Solzhenitsyn experienced freedom for the first time at Riazan in what he regarded as paradise even though his salary was small—50 rubles a month. But thanks to his wife's income, the couple was able to rent a three-room apartment in a run-down two-story house on Proyezd Yablochkova.

A correspondent for the news agency APN who visited Riazan at the end of 1962, reported that the house had a small garden in which Solzhenitsyn enjoyed working and had planted some cherry trees.

In reality, however, the living conditions were far from idyllic. Zhorez Medvedev writes in his book on science policy in the Soviet Union that the apartment was damp and unhealthy and that Solzhenitsyn was very unhappy with it.

According to the APN correspondent, Solzhenitsyn was a very popular teacher. The correspondent says that Solzhenitsyn's colleagues regarded him as an extraordinarily skillful teacher with a thorough education. His students, who were interviewed, stated that Solzhenitsyn gave interesting lectures and expressed himself well. His colleagues, however, saw him as a reserved man who avoided visiting people and who had very few friends. But they stressed his other qualities such as punctuality, determination, energy and self-discipline. In *The First Circle,* Solzhenitsyn describes his *alter ego,* Gleb Nerzhin, as an extremely humble person and schoolmaster.

Solzhenitsyn was an eager amateur photographer and directed a class in photography in the school where he taught. He often went on long bicycle rides with his wife during their summer vacation, and he would take a lot of photographs. One of these long rides is described in *Zakhar-Kalita,* the last of his stories to be published in the Soviet Union.

Nobody, however, knew about his literary work. As a matter of fact, he kept it a secret to all except his wife, until 1961.

The Rehabilitation

On February 6, 1957 his case was reopened by the Supreme Court. The rehabilitation protocol that was smuggled out to the West, reads:

"DECISION BY THE SUPREME COURT OF
THE USSR No. 4n-083/57

The Military Collegium of the Supreme Court of the USSR, composed of the justices, Colonel Dolotsev and Colonel Konov, and presided over by Chief Justice Borisoglebsky has, at a meeting on February 6, 1957, studied the appeal by the Military Chief Prosecutor against a decree by the NKVD's Special Commission of July 7, 1945, on the basis of which, in accordance with sections 58:10 paragraph 2 and 58:11 of the Criminal Code of the RSFSR, a sentence of eight years confinement in a correction camp was pronounced against Solzhenitsyn, Aleksandr Isaevich, born 1918 at Kislovodsk, and having an academic education. Prior to his arrest, he served as a Battery Commander, participating in the war against the German Fascist Armies and was awarded the Order of the Patriotic War (second grade) and the Red Star."

After hearing Comrade Konov's report and a statement by the assistant Military Chief Prosecutor, Colonel Terekhov, who requested the approval of the appeal, the Collegium stipulated the following:

"Solzhenitsyn has been accused of pursuing anti-Soviet propaganda among his friends, and of taking action toward forming an anti-Soviet organization."

The Military Chief Prosecutor suggested in his appeal that

the decree by the Special Commission concerning Solzhenitsyn be annulled and the case withdrawn due to lack of evidence of criminal action. The following motives were given:

"The arguments in this case clearly show that Solzhenitsyn, in his diary and in letters to a friend, N. D. Vitkevich, although he expressed his opinion on the truth of Marxism-Leninism, the progress of the Soviet Revolution in our nation and the inevitability of its victory in the entire world, he also spoke against Stalin's person and wrote about the artistic and ideological flaws in the works of many Soviet writers and about the unreal atmosphere prevailing in many of them. He has also written that our works of art have failed in giving the readers of the bourgeois world a satisfying and multi-faceted explanation for the inevitability of the victory of the Soviet Army and the Soviet People and that our literary works do not offer any resistance against the slander by the bourgeois world against our nation.

These statements by Solzhenitsyn are no evidence of criminal behavior.

In the verification of Solzhenitsyn's plea, hearings were arranged with the following persons: Reshetovskaya, Simonyan and Simonyants, in the presence of whom Solzhenitsyn allegedly had made anti-Soviet statements. These persons characterized Solzhenitsyn as a Soviet patriot and denied that he carried on anti-Soviet conversations.

Solzhenitsyn's military dossier and a report from Captain Melnikow, who served together with him, clearly indicate that Solzhenitsyn, from 1942 until his arrest, served on different fronts in the Great Patriotic War, fought bravely for the Fatherland, more than once, demonstrated personal courage and inspired devotion in his unit. Solzhenitsyn's Battery was the best in the unit as far as discipline and fighting ability go.

On the basis of the evidence mentioned above the Military Chief Prosecutor considers the sentence against Solzhenitsyn incorrect and requests at the same time that the case be dismissed in accordance with section 4:5 of the Criminal Code of the RSFSR.

After examination of the facts of the case, the material investigation and the conformity of the statements of the official appeal, and also, taking into account the fact that Solzhenitsyn's actions are not criminal and the request that his case should be dismissed for lack of evidence, the Military Collegium of the USSR decides that the decree by the NKVD's Special Commission of July 7, 1945 regarding Solzhenitsyn, Aleksandr Isaevich, is annulled and that the case, due to lack of evidence, is dismissed in accordance with section 4:5 of the Criminal Code of the RSFSR."

The Slovakian author Pavel Licko maintains that the three lawyers were the first judges Solzhenitsyn had ever been confronted with in his entire life. They were also the first people to read *One Day in the Life of Ivan Denisovich*. According to Licko, Solzhenitsyn recited the novel to them, evidently as a document for the defense. This, however, seems highly improbable, not to say naive, since the story was not autobiographical and certainly did not contain anything unknown to these three experts on the practice of law during Stalin's era. In spite of its literary qualities it could hardly be relevant to the legal aspects of the case. There is also every indication that Solzhenitsyn completed the novel much later.

Neither do any available documents confirm Licko's statement that Solzhenitsyn was acquitted although he regarded himself as guilty of the "crime" for which he had been sentenced in 1945—that is to say, the criticism of Stalin—though this sort of criticism was in fact liable to punishment. Besides, the rehabilitation document shows that Solzhenitsyn himself had demanded a new trial and that the Military Prosecutor had made the appeal after that. Licko's statement was later used in the slander campaign against Solzhenitsyn as evidence that he was not innocent.

The Debut

Writing in secrecy eventually became intolerable. According to his friends, Solzhenitsyn felt a growing need for readers and particularly critics. After the 22nd Party Congress at which Aleksandr Tvardovsky, the poet, in a very promising speech, called on the writers to write "the whole truth", Solzhenitsyn decided to take the risk and send *One Day in the Life of Ivan Denisovich* to Tvardovsky's magazine *Novy Mir*.

More or less by chance, Tvardovsky happened to notice the manuscript in the big bunch of mail that reached the magazine daily. He read some parts with growing surprise and saw that the writing, in an almost miraculous way, met all the brave demands for truthfulness he himself had emphasized in his address to the Party Congress. He brought the manuscript home with the intention of completing it in bed. He later wrote of what he experienced at that moment:

"And suddenly, I felt that I just could not go on reading without doing anything. I got out of bed and put on my best suit, a white shirt and my best pair of shoes. Thus dressed, I sat there reading a new classic".

Even at this stage Tvardovsky was prepared to put his personal prestige at stake for the publication of this manuscript which, he realized at once, would have the impact of an earthquake and would excite ideological passions. In a letter to Konstantin Fedin, the First Secretary of the Union of Soviet Writers, which was published only outside the Soviet Union, Tvardovsky reveals that he sent copies of the manuscript to several established writers holding high positions in the Party—such as Mikhail Sholokhov—asking their opinion.

Fedin also received the manuscript for the same purpose.

Considering Fedin's bitter pronouncements later and his uncompromising behaviour in the Solzhenitsyn Affair, it is interesting to note that Tvardovsky remarks in his letter that Fedin's "very praising evaluation of the manuscript by the unknown author was of particular importance for its fate". Tvardovsky emphasizes that when turning to Nikita Khrushchev to pursuade him to sanction its publication, he had especially referred to Fedin's positive opinion. Aleksandr Tvardovsky apparently also referred to Sholokhov, the sacrosanct, who soon enough would turn into one of Solzhenitsyn's most unobstructed opponents. In his letter to Fedin, Tvardovsky reveals that Sholokhov at that time "expressed a very favorable opinion of *One Day in the Life of Ivan Denisovich* and asked me to forward his congratulations to the author of the novel". This was considered unique in literary circles since nobody could recall a single occasion on which Sholokhov had expressed an appreciative opinion on any talented living author.

Khrushchev became—for non-literary reasons though—extremely enthusiastic and promised to support Tvardosky. But he apparently did not consider himself entirely able to decide this matter—the publishing of *One Day in the Life of Ivan Denisovich* implied a hardening of the Party's anti-Stalinist line, which, as a matter of fact, came in handy for him, but he had to put the matter before the Presidium. Proof-sheets of the novel were therefore sent to the members of the Party Presidium and apparently, also to other figures in key positions in the Party apparatus. After an evidently extensive debate on Party principles in the top Party leadership Khrushchev pulled his line through and Tvardovsky was able to go ahead with the publication. On November 3, 1962, six weeks after the typesetting and about a year after Solzhenitsyn had sent in the manuscript, the editor of *Novy Mir* signed the document approving the eleventh issue of *Novy Mir* to be printed in an edition of 96,900 copies.

Tvardosky certainly did risk his unique personal prestige at this time by writing an introduction which he headlined: "In Place of a Foreword":

The subject matter of Aleksandr Solzhenitsyn's novel is unusual in Soviet Literature. It echoes the unhealthy phenomena in our life associated with the period of the personality cult, now exposed and rejected by the Party. Although these events are so recent in point of time, they seem very remote to us. But whatever the past was like, we in the present must not be indifferent to it. Only by going into its consequences fully, courageously, and truthfully can we guarantee a complete and irrevocable break with all those things that cast a shadow over the past. This is what N. S. Khrushchev meant when he said in his memorable concluding address at the Twenty-second Congress: 'It is our duty to go carefully into all aspects of all matters connected with the abuse of power. In time we must die, for we are all mortal, but as long as we go on working we can and must clarify many things and tell the truth to the Party and the People. . . . This must be done to prevent such things from happening in the future.'

One Day in the Life of Ivan Denisovich is not a book of memoirs in the ordinary sense of the word. It does not consist merely of notes on the author's personal experiences and his memories of them, although only personal experience could have given the novel such an authentic quality. It is a work of art. And it is the way in which the raw material is handled that gives it its outstanding value as a testimony and makes it an artistic document, the possibility of which had hitherto seemed unlikely on the basis of 'concrete material'.

In Solzhenitsyn the reader will not find an exhaustive account of that historical period marked in particular by the year 1937, so bitter in all our memories. The theme of *One Day* is inevitably limited by the time and place of the action and by the boundaries of the world to which the hero was confined. One day in the life of Ivan Denisovich Shukhov, a prisoner in a forced labor camp, as described by Aleksandr Solzhenitsyn (this is the author's first appearance in print) unfolds as a picture of exceptional vividness and truthfulness about the nature of man. It is this above all that gives the work its unique impact. The reader could easily imagine many of the people shown here in these tragic circumstances as fighting at the front or working on postwar reconstruction. They are the same sort of people, but they have been exposed by fate to a cruel ordeal—not only physical but moral.

The author of this novel does not go out of his way to emphasize the arbitrary brutality which was a consequence of the breakdown of Soviet legality. He has taken a very ordinary day—from reveille to lights out—in the life of a prisoner. But this ordinary day cannot fail to fill the reader's heart with bitterness and pain at the fate of these people who come to life before his eyes and seem so close to him in the pages of this book. The author's greatest achievement, however, is that this bitterness and pain do not convey a feeling of utter despair. On the contrary. The effect of this novel, which is so unusual for its honesty and harrowing truth, is to unburden our minds of things thus far unspoken, but which had to be said. It thereby strengthens and ennobles us.

This stark tale shows once again that today there is no aspect of our life that cannot be dealt with and faithfully described in Soviet Literature. Now it is only a question of how much talent the writer brings to it. There is another very simple lesson to be learned from this novel. If the theme of a work is truly significant, if it is faithful to the great truths of life, and if it is deeply human in its presentation of even the most painful subjects, then it cannot help finding the appropriate form of expression. The style of *One Day* is vivid and original in its unpretentiousness and down-to-earth simplicity. It is quite un-self-conscious and thereby gains great inner strength and dignity.

I do not want to anticipate reader's judgements of this short work, but I myself have not the slightest doubt that it marks the appearance on the literary scene of a new, original, and mature talent.

It may well be that the author's use—however sparing and to the point—of certain words and expressions typical of the setting in which the hero lived and worked may offend a particularly fastidious taste. But all in all, *One Day* is a work for which one has such a feeling of gratitude to the author that one's greatest wish is that this gratitude be shared by other readers.

Aleksandr Tvardovsky

About November 20 the distribution of the 11th edition of *Novy Mir* began in Moscow and Leningrad. Excited, sensational rumors spread in literary circles in Moscow days before. The copies in the bookstores—only a small amount since the magazine by tradition relies on subscriptions—were immediately sold out. Solzhenitsyn's novel hit the capital like a bombshell—and this happened at a time when the members of the Central Committee had gathered for an important plenary session. The central press could not wait to declare the unknown upstart a genius and the most remarkable thing was that *Pravda* and the most Party oriented newspapers led this unusual panegyrical campaign.

A chronological summary, month by month and occasionally even day by day, of the dramatic events full of conflicts that occurred in the cultural field at that time, gives a conception of the fierceness of the polarization.

While this polarization goes ahead Solzhenitsyn's opponents as well as supporters could pick new and sharper arguments out of the short stories (*An Incident at Krechetovka Station, Matryona's House* and *For the Good of the Cause*) that were published in the January and July 1963 editions of *Novy Mir.*

In 1962, the fall semester for the Intermediate School at Riazan ended on 28 December, and Solzhenitsyn left the teaching profession for good. A few weeks later he was accepted as a member of the Union of Soviet Writers despite lame protests from the local organization in Riazan. His acceptance by the union was unique in two ways: the decision was reached in a great hurry, and secondly, it was made without consideration for the opinion of the primary organization—the authors of Riazan.

The Controversy Starts
Chronological Summary

In the last few days of November and the first days of December a long line of unusually warm reviews of *One Day in the Life of Ivan Denisovich* was published in the central press in Moscow. The headlines were all pathetic and had a slight touch of sensationalism. On November 18, even before the story was available, this panegyrical series had been started by the author Konstantin Simonov, in the Government newspaper *Izvestia*. His article was headlined: "About the Past in the Name of The Future". On November 22, the mouthpiece of the Writers' Unions, *Literaturnaya Gazeta*, published Grigori Baklanov's now almost classic review entitled "In Order that This Will Never be Repeated". Baklanov wrote that since the publication of *One Day in the Life of Ivan Denisovich*, "it has become very evident that it will never be possible again to write in the way we wrote until recently".

The following day the Party newspaper *Pravda* joined the chorus by publishing the review "In the Name of Truth, In the Name of Justice", by the normally highly conformist critic, Viktor Yermilov. On November 28, Aleksandr Dymshits wrote in *Literatura i zhizn* (*Literature and Life*), the medium of the Russian Writers' Union. Important articles about the novel were later published in the magazine *Ogonyok*. Notable among them was N. Kruzhkov's "So it Was, So Will It Never be Again". Other articles appeared in the Union publication *Trud,* such as V. Litvinov's "Yes, the Whole Truth Will Come Out". The

headlines of these centrally inspired articles give a clear indication of the political expectations at that time.

In an address which has never been made public, Khrushchev
allegedly told the Central Committee that he personally sanctioned the publication of Yevgeny Yevtushenko's poem: "The
Heirs of Stalin" and had intervened for the publication of *One
Day in the Life of Ivan Denisovich*. He reportedly stressed that
other Soviet leaders during a debate had raised objections or
suggested exclusions. However, he had rejected these suggestions with the motivation that "nobody has the right to change
the writer's version".

Yevgeny Yevtushenko confirms in *Autobiographie précoce,*
which was published in Paris in 1963, without the consent of
the Soviet censorship agency, that he sent "The Heirs of
Stalin" to Khrushchev personally. Yevtushenko continues: "We
also owe Khrushchev credit for his intervention on behalf of
Solzhenitsyn's remarkable story *One Day in the Life of Ivan
Denisovich,* the publication of which is a true mile-stone in the
development of our Literature".

On November 26, the "modernistic" exhibition highlighting
the works of the sculptor Ernst Neizvestny, was opened in Elya
Belutin's studio at Bolshaya Kommunistichskaya Ulitsa in
Moscow. The exhibition, which on the opening day, was visited
by hundreds of specially invited people belonging to the cultural
elite, was generally—but apparently naively—regarded as a
"turning point" for the experimental art forms. Three days
later, a minor exhibition of the works of the painters who had
exhibited in Belutin's studio, was stopped. The paintings had
already been hung on the walls of the Young Communist
League's new hotel "Yunost", but were banned only a few
hours before the scheduled opening. At the same time Belutin
was ordered to send the works that had been on exhibition in
his studio to the central exhibition hall—The Manège—at the
Kremlin. For some time The Manège had been the scene of a
widely mentioned and a much frequented exhibition arranged
to celebrate the 30th anniversary of Moscow's Artists' Union.

The Manège exhibits included many works by controversial

painters, including modernists of the twenties and thirties such as the cubist Robert Falk, whose "Rehabilitation" Ilya Ehrenburg had advocated so eagerly on many occasions, especially in his memoirs *Men, Years, Life.*

A great cultural event in Moscow during these weeks of optimism was a big poetry reading night at the Lenin stadium at Luzhniki on November 30 when poets like Andrei Voznesensky and Boris Slutsky recited controversial poems to fifteen thousand listeners. The militia was called out to handle the crowds of people who had not managed to get tickets. The incident illustrates the hunger and enthusiasm the youth in particular felt for the new trend.

December

Aleksandr Solzhenitsyn was still a practically anonymous author. Soviet as well as foreign journalists now felt that this *débutant,* who had become world-famous practically overnight—the night of November 20 to November 21—was inaccessible.

Toward the end of November, the Teacher's Magazine (*Uchitelskaya Gazeta*) in Moscow sent a journalist to Riazan hoping that Solzhenitsyn could at least be approached in his capacity as a teacher. But Solzhenitsyn refused to give him an interview. The reporter, N. Kashkadamov, noticeably impressed, wrote that Solzhenitsyn had made up his mind not to make any statements to the press—"and as always, he is keeping his promise", according to the article which was published on December 1.

The same day Nikita Khrushchev, followed by the whole Party Presidium and a retinue of representatives of the artists' organisations, visited the Manège exhibition. He was, according to several witnesses, in an excellent mood on his arrival. But gradually his looks turned gloomy and he launched into a vicious attack against the older, "modernist" artists (particularly Robert Falk) as well as against the younger "abstractionists" and the sculptor Ernst Neizvestny.

The visit marked the beginning of a long and grotesque confrontation with "modernism" in all its forms—a confrontation in which talent was indiscriminately buried with diletantism in the same mass-grave.

This campaign was, in the months that ensued, extended to the entire cultural life and the ideology, in particular the attitude to the Stalinist heritage. To cap this fierce debate, Khrushchev's own politics were declared bankrupt.

On December 8, the *Moskovskaya Pravda,* the newspaper of the Party organization in Moscow, published a review of *One Day in the Life of Ivan Denisovich* which superficially seemed positive. The review, Ivan Chicherov's "In the Name of the Future", was in fact a well concealed attack of the kind that would later become frequent. He wrote:

> "What worries me in this story is the attitude of the common people, and all these camp inmates, toward the intellectuals who, all the time, experience (and even in the camp continue discussing) Eisenstein and Meyerhold, film and literature, Yuri Zavadsky's new play . . . . Sometimes one has a feeling of an ironic, occasionally scornful, attitude of the author toward these people."

The criticism was undoubtedly absurd and unjust. However, it turned out to be extremely vigorous and even became the model for coming attacks.

On December 17, the Party leaders met with 400 chosen cultural personalities of the nation in a palace on the Lenin Hill in Moscow.

Nikita Khrushchev and his cultural ideologist, Leonid Ilyichov, as well as some others, indicated in their speeches a coming restraint of cultural policy. The debate was based on the two art exhibitions, Ehrenburg's memoirs (*Men, Years, Life,* which had been running as a serial in *Novy Mir* since 1960) and several other controversial works by writers, artists and movie makers. Khrushchev's address to the meeting was not published. It seems Aleksandr Solzhenitsyn was present that day since Tvardovsky wrote that Khrushchev "introduced him at the meeting".

However, Ilyichov's speech was given extensive coverage and long excerpts were published. He disclosed that groups of intellectuals had written to Khrushchev after his visit to the Manège exhibition and also, during the press campaign that followed against several experimental artists and outspoken writers. They urged him to stop what they saw as an attempt to revive Stalinist methods against dissenters. Ilyichov extensively quoted one of these letters, however, without revealing that it had been signed by prominent citizens including the Nobel Prize laureates Igor Tamm and Nikolai Semenov, famous writers like Konstantin Simonov, Illya Ehrenburg and Kornei Chukovsky, the composer Dmitri Shostakovich, and the movie director Mikhail Romm.

At this meeting Aleksandr Solzhenitsyn was still a *protégé* of the Party or at least of the Party leader. Ilyichov declared:

"The Party supports the healthy, vigorous currents in the Socialist realism. Artistically and politically strong works truthfully and bravely exposing the arbitrariness in the days of the personality cult have been published lately with the consent of the Central Committee. I need only mention A. Solzhenitsyn's story *One Day in the Life of Ivan Denisovich.*"

From December 24 to 26 the leading ideologists of the Party again conferred in Moscow with 140 intellectuals.

January, 1963

The magazine *Don,* a publication for authors in the circle of Mikhail Sholokhov, published in its first edition of the year, F. Chapchakhov's insidious review of *One Day in the Life of Ivan Denisovich* entitled "Numbers and People". The writer wondered:

"Nevertheless one is inclined to ask: 'do those our critics, without reservation, accept as accurate Shukhov's person as described in the story?"

On January 11, Lidya Fomenko sharpened the criticism against *One Day in the Life of Ivan Denisovich* in the publication of the Russian Writers' Union *Literaturnaya Rossiya.* She claimed that the novel

"does not give the whole truth of those times . . . . Despite the artistic refinement and the bitter truth, Solzhenitsyn's story does not disclose all the dialectics of that time. A passionate 'No!' to Stalinist order is cried out here. Shukhov and others have preserved their human nature. The story, however, does not reach up to the philosophical level of that period, to a broader generalization that would cover the controversial tendencies of the epoch. Fortunately, the cult was not as almighty as Stalin himself, Shukhov, and almost everybody else, thought at that time. The powerful force of the People was attributed to one single man and so this inexhaustible creative power performed his big, historical deed".

Lidya Fomenko finds a lack of balance in the description of "the creative work of that time and the law violations". Rather, she praises Georgi Shelest's "The Golden Nugget" as having obtained much better balance. That was a "conservative" story of a prison camp which was published a few weeks after Solzhenitsyn's novel. In that story the political prisoners never for a moment wavered in their political faith, not even under the most repulsive conditions.

On January 25 *Literaturnaya Rossiya* published a *réportage* by Viktor Bukhanov about Solzhenitsyn. In reference to his unsuccessful effort to interview Solzhenitsyn, Bukhanov stressed his "unique self-discipline, industriousness, seclusiveness and profound shyness". Bukhanov also wrote of Solzhenitsyn's cancer, which had been halted by "brave surgery"—a big exaggeration since the operation at the camp hospital at Ekibastuz failed. (Solzhenitsyn was cured by radium treatment in Tashkent.) The Soviet journalist also stressed Solzhenitsyn's unusual integrity—he was pictured as totally indifferent to money and had, for "the past five years", (that is, after the rehabilitation) been living on a teacher's salary of 50 rubles a month.

Bukhanov also mentioned the fact that Solzhenitsyn had spent New Year's Day of 1963 with a group of actors from the Sovremennik Theater in Moscow. A short time earlier he had read to them his new play, *The Love Girl and the Innocent*. Bukhanov assumed in the article that the play was to be produced by the Sovremennik Theater. An agreement was in fact reached by the author and the theater shortly before the end of the year.

January was in many ways a month of events for Solzhenitsyn. *An Incident at Krechetovka Station* and *Matryona's House* were published in *Novy Mir* in its first issue of the year. It was reported that *One Day* was being translated into Estonian, Latvian and Lithuanian and was going to be published in the other Peoples' Republics. At the end of the month *One Day* was published in book form. 100,000 copies were printed by the publishing house Sovjetsky Pisatel. The novel magazine

Roman-Gazeta carried the story in its first edition of the year, printing 700,000 copies.

February-March

February was marked by a noticeable lull in the debate. However, criticism, often couched in generally kind and patronizing phrases, began to appear.

On March 2 the writer Vadim Kozhevnikov attacked *Matryona's House* in *Literaturnaya Gazeta*—the first warning of the magazine's changed policy. At the end of 1962, the editor, V. A. Kosolapov, who had been subjected to bitter criticism for publishing Yevtushenko's poem about antisemitism ("Babi Yar"), resigned and was succeeded by Aleksandr Chakovsky. Kozhevnikov's article, "Comrades in Arms", was undoubtedly a result of the new editorship and a reversion toward conformism, Kozhevnikov dismissed *Matryona's House* as a simplified story about people "without a non-too-serious content". He repeated Lidya Fomenko's accusation that Solzhenitsyn has a deficient sense of historical truth. Kozhevnikov used the same method as Fomenko did: he compared *Matryona's House* to a novel by Boris Polevoi (*Na dikom brege . . .*) which was mildly critical of the society. The intentions were obvious: to create the impression that Solzhenitsyn's first novel was an accidental success; he had not, after all, fulfilled the people's expectations of him later on; in fact, he had no depth and serenity; other authors wrote better about similar problems . . . .

On March 7 and 8, the most prominent Soviet leaders met with six hundred cultural personalities in the Sverdlov Hall in the Kremlin. The tone was sharpened furthermore by Ilyichov who strongly attacked Ilya Ehrenburg for his efforts to rehabilitate artists and writers who were suppressed during Stalin's era and in particular, his slogan about "peaceful co-existence" between the different schools of art.

At this meeting Khrushchev made a sensational effort to save Stalin's honor on several decisive points. But at the same time, he refused to withdraw his protection for the "de-Stalinists" he earlier supported:

"In their creative work in the last few years, writers and artists have paid a great deal of attention to the chapter of life in the Soviet society connected with the Stalin cult. All this is consequent and there are many reasons for doing so. Several works have been published that reflect the realities in the Soviet Union truthfully in line with the Party's position. Good examples are Aleksandr Tvardovsky's *Beyond the Beyond,* Aleksandr Solzhenitsyn's *One Day in the Life of Ivan Denisovich,* certain poems by Yevgeny Yevtushenko and Grigori Chukhrai's film *The Clear Sky.*"

Khrushchev added that· "the Party supports artistic works that are truthful regardless of what negative aspects of reality they deal with, as long as they benefit the people in their efforts of building the new society."

Probably trying to balance the opposing groups and prevent a serious split, Khrushchev at the same time praised Mikhail Sholokhov as a brave fighter against Stalinist outrages during the collectivizing of agriculture in the Don area. This homage, as well as the attack in the magazine *Don* a short time earlier, indicate that Sholokhov, by this time, had been won over to the anti-Solzhenitsyn camp.

Sometime in the middle of the month the head of the State Movie Committee, Alexei Romanov, spoke at a meeting of moviemakers in Moscow. In the discussion following the address bitter criticism allegedly was voiced against the most prominent "revisionist" publications, particularly *Novy Mir.*

Toward the end of March the Union of Soviet Writers held an important plenary session. On March 22, *Komsomolskaya Pravda* published a speech by Komsomol's first secretary, Sergei Pavlov, who was also a member of the Central Committee. Pavlov was the first high Party official to attack Solzhenitsyn publicly. His speech was also nearly polemical against Khrushchev's statements at the Sverdlov Hall. This was the first indisputable indication of opposition to Khrushchev himself:

"At the eighth International Youth and Students Festival we were asked by the American, French and Italian delegations: 'How come that we meet nice Soviet people in real life when certain Soviet books are about a different kind of people?' And it is true— one only has to read I. Ehrenburg's memoirs, A. Yashin's *Wedding in Vologda,* V. Nekrasov's letters from his travels, V. Aksyonov's *Halfway to the Moon,* A. Solzhenitsyn's *Matryona's House* and V. Voinovich's *I Want to Be Honest*—all published in the magazine *Novy Mir.* These works invoke such pessimism and hopelessness that I am afraid they might mislead a person who lacks knowledge of our life. *Novy Mir* happens to publish such works with unaccountable persistence".

On March 30, the writer Viktor Poltoratsky attacked *Matryona's House* in the Government newspaper *Izvestia* in an insidious manner. He even questioned Solzhenitsyn's honesty: "A. Solzhenitsyn is a talented, and I believe, honest writer".

Poltoratsky then tried energetically to prove that Solzhenitsyn is not honest but has one-sidedly chosen to write on the shady side of Soviet life and old-fashioned, unrepresentative collective farms.

April

Literaturnaya Gazeta continued during April to publish speeches held at the writers' meeting in Moscow the previous month. On April 2, a statement by the author Mikhail Sokolov was quoted:

> "Why is it that in the pages of *Novy Mir* only we find first one, then a second and now a third work that strikes us dumb: Ehrenburg's memoirs, Nekrasov's notes, Solzhenitsyn's stories and so on?
> Obviously the Party's direction of the publications, the newspapers and even the Writers' Union itself is far from satisfying.
> Comrade Tvardovsky is an important poet, but the editor Tvardovsky makes mistakes. Let us talk to him about them hoping that he won't make new ones.
> But it is striking that when the publisher Tvardovsky is being criticized he keeps quiet."

This contribution to the debate also gives clear evidence of Khrushchev's already waning influence; even a totally insignificant writer was able to question his evaluations expressed in an authoritative "party voice". Sokolov demanded stricter censorship (which Khrushchev ignored by going through with the publication of *One Day in the Life of Ivan Denisovich*) and criticized as "a mistake" that Solzhenitsyn's stories were printed even if they had Khrushchev's blessing.

In mid-April the main publication of the "dogmatists," *Okchabr* appeared with an all-out attack against everything Solzhenitsyn had published including *An Incident at Krechetovka Station.* The attack was launched by the critic N. Sergovantsev. Despite the fact that Khrushchev, only shortly before, had stated that *One Day in the Life of Ivan Denisovich* truthfully and in accordance with the Party's position reflected real life in the Soviet Union under Stalin's rule, the critic Sergovantsev dismissed Ivan Denisovich Shukhov as an intellectually and morally limited, and generally doubtful, fiction figure. He also rejected *An Incident at Krechetovka Station* as being profoundly unsatisfactory and without historical perspectives. He implied that Solzhenitsyn was regarding the Soviet Union as a society of classes with "poor" and "rich" people, with the former in one way or another being suppressed by the latter.

Sergovantsev made the following accusation on ideological grounds against *An Incident at Krechetovka Station:*

"Because of his imaginatively limited view of life and lack of understanding in objective historical processes, A. Solzhenitsyn attributes to our social order and the people who have been brought up in it, characteristics that in no way are essential to this reality and to the people who grew up under these conditions. The author has not understood or wanted to understand this. That is the reason for his distrust of the true reality and his rejection of its humanistic fundamentals."

May

One month after Mikhail Sokolov's attack against the editorial policy of Tvardovsky, the editor broke his silence by answering, by mail, questions put by Henry Shapiro, chief correspondent in Moscow, of the American News Agency, UPI. The interview was published on May 12 by the Party newspaper *Pravda* and was later carried, in a slightly different version, as an editorial in the fourth edition of *Novy Mir.*

Tvardovsky commented on several cultural and political questions but particularly on Aleksandr Solzhenitsyn. He characterized *One Day in the Life of Ivan Denisovich* as "in my opinion, a very important and significant phenomenon" and continued:

"It is not only because it is based on a certain, specific material and shows the characteristics of hostility to the People in occurrences connected with the consequences of the Stalin cult, but also because its aesthetic structure confirms the unchanging importance of artistic truthfulness and decisively turns against false formalistic and modernistic whims.

My opinion is that *One Day* is one of those literary phenomena after the appearance of which it is impossible to discuss a literary problem or literary fact without using this unusual piece of work as a measure.

I will never forget the way N. S. Khrushchev reacted to Solzhenitsyn's story—to its hero, who preserves the dignity and beauty of a working man in inhuman conditions, to the truthfulness of the story, to the writer's attitude to the bitter and hard realities. At the first meeting (with the cultural elite) Nikita Sergeyevich Khrushchev mentioned Solzhenisyn's name in his speech and introduced him to everyone who was present in the Reception Hall on the Lenin Hill.

If it were necessary to demonstrate the broad-mindedness, on literature and art, of our Central Committee, it would be more than enough to mention the fact that it approved of A. Solzhenitsyn's story".

At the end of the exchange, which was full of such unintentionally ironic twists, Tvardovsky told Shapiro that *Novy Mir* was expecting a new work by Solzhenitsyn. Later controversies revealed that Tvardovsky had the first part of *Cancer Ward* in mind.

The Summer

The dispute around Solzhenitsyn continued throughout the spring and the summer but in relatively moderate terms. The Central Committee met in mid-June. This time the greatest attention was given to the conflict with China; however, cultural problems were still discussed peripherally. In addressing the plenary meeting, Khrushchev, for the first time, failed to mention Solzhenitsyn by name although he spoke about the anti-Stalinist literature, for example, Tvardovsky's poem.

The 39th edition of the magazine *Ogoniok* carried a new attack against *One Day in the Life of Ivan Denisovich*. The reviewer used the tested but absurd method of playing down Solzhenitsyn's story by overwhelmingly praising a fairly indifferent suspense novel by I. Lazutin as the following line shows:

"Contrary to A. Solzhenitsyn's story *One Day in the Life of Ivan Denisovich* Lazutin's novel shows many facets of real life".

In the summer an international symposium on Literature was held in Leningrad. Aleksandr Tvardovsky was one of the speakers. Trying not to modify the importance of the controversy around Solzhenitsyn's person, he said in a statement later published in *Literaturnaya Gazeta* on August 10:

"Regardless of one's attitude to this talent, it is impossible to study any new literary events without making comparisons with this artist."

A new controversy arose from Solzhenitsyn's short story *For the Good of the Cause* in the July edition of *Novy Mir*. On August 3. *Literaturnaya Gazeta's* critic, Yuri Barabash, called the story "a failure".

The Fall

The attacks against Solzhenitsyn grew sharper in the months of late fall and early winter. On October 19 *Literaturnaya Gazeta's* critic N. Seliverstov went so far as to insist that Solzhenitsyn had violated the laws of social realism by "having mechanically transferred the tradition of critical (19th century) realism to socialistic bases: this was considered a "great danger".

The bitterest attack against Solzhenitsyn thus far was launched by V. Chalmayev in the tenth edition of the publication *Oktyabr*. Chalmayev's main target was Solzhenitsyn's *For the Good of the Cause* in which the writer is said to demonstrate "an extraordinary incompetence in interpreting a contemporary material of realities". Besides, a provincial newspaper, *Kazakhstanskaya Pravda,* had already, at the beginning of the month, published a letter by a former camp prisoner, Aleksandr Gudzenko, against *One Day in the Life of Ivan Denisovich* in which Solzhenitsyn is accused of distorting facts and giving a gloomy picture of life in a camp.

In its tenth edition, *Novy Mir,* however, made a counter-attack by giving three readers the opportunity to defend *For the Good of the Cause* against Yuri Barabash's criticism.

This forced the debate to escalate. *Okchabr's* editor Vsevolod Kochetov, who so far had been very anxious to keep himself out of the debate, made in the November issue an all-out attack against Tvardovsky's and *Novy Mir's* persistent defense of Solzhenitsyn as being "a new Tolstoy". In the same issue, the critic A. Dremov, violently disputed Tvardovsky's statement on Solzhenitsyn at the symposium in Leningrad. The literary debate rolled on and off in different publications.

At this point a scandal occurred.

On December 12, *Literaturnaya Gazeta* had carelessly accused *Novy Mir* of publishing only letters from their readers with positive statements about Solzhenitsyn. The magazine indicated that Tvardovsky silenced critical voices. On December 26, the Editorial Board of *Novy Mir* responded with an open letter in *Literaturnaya Gazeta.* According to this, *Novy Mir* had altogether received 58 letters about *For the Good of the Cause.* A total of 55 had been positive, two had contained complaints about the style and one had been totally negative but so slanderous that it could not have been published.

Novy Mir, however, made the sensational disclosure that 12 of the positive letters were copies. The originals had been sent to *Literaturnaya Gazeta* which had refused to publish them!

The Fight About the Lenin Prize

The reason for this unique—by Soviet standards—polemic between two newspapers both of which were official publications of the Union of Soviet Writers, soon became clear.

On December 28, *Literaturnaya Gazeta* published an official statement by the Committee for the Lenin Prize for Literature. According to this, *Novy Mir,* together with the State Central Archives of Literature and Art had recommended *One Day in the Life of Ivan Denisovich* for the Lenin Prize for 1964.

Obviously in an effort to reject *Novy Mir's* counter accusations of being biased, *Literaturnaya Gazeta* published a *positive* letter from a reader on Solzhenitsyn on January 11, 1964.

Shortly thereafter the Government newspaper *Izvestia,* added its bit to the accumulating material by publishing a rather sensational interview in Leningrad with Captain Boris Burkovsky, commander of the cruiser *Aurora,* famous from the Revolution. He disclosed that he, in fact, was identical with Captain Buynovsky in *One Day in the Life of Ivan Denisovich.* Burkovsky therefore dismissed as vulgar the claims by the critics that the persons in Solzhenitsyn's novels are fictitious. He even declared that Solzhenitsyn's story gives an "exact" description of life in the camp.

It began to look as if the wind had shifted once more. On January 30, the Jewish poet Samuil Marshak wrote an utterly flattering article of Solzhenitsyn in the Party newspaper *Pravda.* The event was regarded as especially important since Marshak had been awarded the Lenin Prize for Literature the year before. Some people even saw a reflection of the Party leader behind the article.

In its January issue *Novy Mir* published a brilliant essay by Vladimir Lakshin on the debate about Solzhenitsyn entitled:

"Ivan Denisovich's Friends and Enemies". Because of its unusual intellectual penetration and its unmistakeable support of Solzhenitsyn, the essay itself became controversial in the debate that followed. By attacking Lakshin's essay the conformists tried to get at Solzhenitsyn and the editorial policy of *Novy Mir*. Indirect attacks of this kind were made at different meetings of writers, by men like the author Dmitri Yeremin, General Aleksandr Todorsky and Boris Diakov—a writer who had described his (and Todorsky's) time in a Stalinist camp in a noncontroversial way and whom the conformists therefore tried to use to outplay Solzhenitsyn.

The Yugoslav publicist Mihajlo Mihajlov, who shortly afterwards started to collect material for his controversial book *Moscow Summer, 1964* was told by Lakshin that after the essay "Ivan Denisovich's Friends and Enemies" was published he received up to 150 letters daily from readers. Lakshin's fundamental opinion was *One Day* had been an unfailing test of people's attitude to Stalinism—a thesis which was first introduced by Grigori Baklanov and thereafter was supported by the critic Yuri Karyakin, the editor of *Novy Mir,* Tvardovsky, and others.

At a meeting with the Writers' Union of Moscow, Solzhenitsyn's close friend and fellow prisoner at the "sharashka" at Mavrino, Lev Kopelev, made a passionate speech defending *One Day in the Life of Ivan Denisovich* and suggesting Solzhenitsyn as a candidate for the Lenin Prize. (Kopelev has identified himself as the prototype of Lev Rubin in *The First Circle.*) Solzhenitsyn was also praised in exceptionally eulogistic terms by the old and highly respected author Venyanin Kaverin. At the same meeting, letters from Ilya Ehrenburg and Kornei Chukovsky were read. Both—the last of the great names of the twenties still alive—made statements favoring Solzhenitsyn as a self-evident candidate.

On February 4, the Committee for the Lenin Prize started its formal discussions. Sixteen days later *Literaturnaya Gazeta* reported that 12 out of a total of 19 suggested works had been eliminated. One of the remaining seven was *One Day in the Life of Ivan Denisovich.*

At this point the opponents were ready to launch a new offensive. Once again, the Komsomol leader Sergei Pavlov took the lead. Zhorez Medvedev has stated that Pavlov, in his capacity as a member of the Committee for the Lenin Prize, declared that "A. I. Solzhenitsyn reportedly has served a prison term for crimes and has not been rehabilitated". Pavlov also claimed that Solzhenitsyn had been taken prisoner of war by the Germans.

By these statements Pavlov had guaranteed a negative vote for Solzhenitsyn. When Tvardovsky, who also was a member of the Committee, shortly afterwards managed to show documents proving that Pavlov's statements were false, the Komsomol leader willingly apologized—but already carried his point.

On February 23, the Prize Committee was attacked by Leonid Sobolev in the daily *Sovjetskaya Rossiya*. He accused the committee of having "evidently unjustifiably" dropped the poet Boris Ruchov from the discussion. (Ruchov was the candidate of the conformists; he had been in a prison camp for many years without, for a moment, losing his faith in Stalin's almightiness and justice.) Two days earlier the Government newspaper *Izvestia* had given vent to its irritation by declaring that the Soviet "public" was extremely discontented with dealings of the Prize Committee. Toward the spring, as a result of the heated debate around *Ivan Denisovich* and the strong pressure against the Committee for the Lenin Prize, Nikita Khrushchev no longer dared to risk his personal prestige by giving continued support to Solzhenitsyn.

On April 11, the Party newspaper *Pravda* broke its silence. The Daily summarized the debate around *One Day in the Life of Ivan Denisovich*. "There existed," said *Pravda*, "three different attitudes to the story: a positive, a negative and a third opinion which presumably was the mostly accepted and correct, meaning that *One Day*, despite all its good qualities, "is not to be compared to the kind of outstanding works that are worth the Lenin Prize". In the eyes of ordinary Party members around the nation, this declaration cast a peculiar light on Khrushchev's intervention on behalf of the story.

After *Pravda* had stated this third "Solomon-like" standpoint it was obvious that the Party would only accept a compromise candidate.

Eleven days later, on Lenin's birthday, the prize was awarded. The winner was the Ukrainian prose writer Oles Gonchar ("Tronka"), who is not uninteresting but lacks any broader significance.

At that time rumors began to spread in Moscow that Tvardovsky was going to be removed from the Committee for the Lenin Prize and would resign as the editor of *Novy Mir*. At about the same time Solzhenitsyn had completed *The First Circle* and handed it over to Tvardovsky who accepted it.

The decision of the Prize Committee was the first public demonstration against Nikita Khrushchev's personal prestige.

International Controversies

International undertones were soon heard in the polemics around Aleksandr Solzhenitsyn. The debate reflected in its own way the complicated ideological relations the Soviet Communist Party had with other ruling fraternal parties. A summary showing to which extent Solzhenitsyn's work have been published in other Socialist countries is very illustrative.

In the People's Republic of China, Solzhenitsyn was attacked at an early stage as being a typical exponent of literary revisionism. Consequently, he was neither published there nor in the Socialist countries which are close to the Chinese version of Communism (Albania, North Korea, North Vietnam).

Neither was he published in the nations which had not yet broken with the personality cult: Mongolia, East Germany.

He has not been published in Romania, which in the sixties, always tried to maintain a balance between Peking and Moscow in ideological matters. Probably more surprising is the fact that Solzhenitsyn has also not been published in Poland.

The first Communist nations to translate *One Day in the Life of Ivan Denisovich* (as early as 1963) were Bulgaria, Hungary, Yugoslavia and Czechoslovakia. When the polemics against Solzhenitsyn got underway in the Soviet Union, the publication of the rest of his works was halted in Bulgaria and Hungary, the two nations which have always been very susceptible to ideological signals.

In Czechoslovakia however, the publication was continued in Czech as well as in Slovak. Already, before the fall of Antonin Novotny, three volumes by Solzhenitsyn had been published in Prague and the same number in Bratislava. During

Dubcek's regime excerpts from Solzhenitsyn's "banned" works, *The First Circle* and *Cancer Ward,* appeared in the magazines. After Gustav Husak assumed power, the publication of Solzhenitsyn's works was discontinued.

In Yugoslavia practically all prose works by Aleksandr Solzhenitsyn have been published—even *Cancer Ward* and *The First Circle*—the latter even in a Russian private edition.

Even in the Solzhenitsyn affair, Cuba demonstrated its independence as had been its practice since the late sixties. In 1965 when Solzhenitsyn already belonged to the controversial personalities in his native country, a Cuban publisher came out with *One Day in the Life of Ivan Denisovich.*

Nikita Khrushchev was removed as Party and government leader in a stormy plenary session in October of 1964.

A month earlier, the Prague-based international theoretical magazine *Problemy mira i sotsializma* (*Problems of Peace and Socialism*) had published an essay by the Soviet critic Yuri Karyakin. The events of the following weeks accidentally gave the title of the essay, "An Episode in the Contemporary Battle of Ideas"—an ironic meaning.

Karyakin remarked that the polemics around *One Day in the Life of Ivan Denisovich* have "become a link in the ideological struggle on the international arena".

"Two factors have", he continues, "in fact contributed to the bitterness of the debate: the opposition of the Chinese leaders and the disclosures in the story about 'the extremes' of the Stalin cult."

Karyakin wrote a curious catalogue of accusations against Solzhenitsyn, but by only vaguely hinting at the sources, he—obviously intentionally—gave the impression that similar "Chinese" and "Albanian" valuations had been heard at a closer distance, possibly even in the Soviet Union, by "people who pose as Communists".

Some of these anonymous quotes were sensational—for example, the following statement quoted by Karyakin:

"The story has been written only to satisfy those who implore a liquidation of the consequences of the personality cult and who slander the Socialist society and the leadership of the Party".

This quotation could hardly originate from Chinese, North Korean or Albanian sources since they probably would not have any objections against criticism of the Soviet Party leadership, which Peking and Tirana on the contrary, were urging the Soviet people to overthrow. The quoted statement must have been given orally by a Russian or at least East European source. It may be worthy of note that the same arguments were used five years later by the Writers Union of Riazan when Solzhenitsyn was expelled as a member. Karyakin wrote that these so-called Communists, when attacking the story of N. S. Krushchev, who in his new policy approved of such works which are spreading the poison of the bourgeois ideology, emphasized the link between its publication and the cause of the Soviet Communist Party and the 20th Party Congress.

The excessive international overtones in Karyakin's essay a month before Khrushchev's fall were naturally motivated by the polemics with the Chinese. In the closing paragraph, however, he made such generalizations that his opinions obviously concerned the polarization process as well as the ideological struggle which were taking place in the Soviet Union at that time:

"The plain fact that A. I. Solzhenitsyn's story has been published by the Communists is considered another important victory for the cause of the 20th Party Congress and by their opponents, a defeat. The Marxist critics do not insist that everybody who does not consider it (the story) of great significance, must be a supporter of the personality cult or conservative, reactionary and so forth. But the Marxist criticism stands up without compromises against anyone who claims that this is an anti-Soviet, anti-Socialist work, hostile to the Party. The logic of real life and the class struggle shows that the longer and the more one hates and fears this story—as one hates and fears a living and strong enemy—the prouder the author can be of such a hatred."

Karyakin's article which probably was written in the summer or earlier, reflected the struggle of ideas in the Soviet Union during this period prior to Khrushchev's fall. Once more, Solzhenitsyn's story was used for testing the ideological struggle. Karyakin's attitude was evidently controversial. He was later expelled from the Communist Party but was back in the Party's good graces in 1968.

There have been different reports that Nikita Khruschchev's intervention on behalf of *"One Day in the Life of Ivan Denisovich"* was mentioned on the long list of offenses presented to him at the plenary session in October at which his removal was decided upon. There are many things indicating that these reports were true but they have not yet been confirmed. (Tvardovsky, who had been playing such an important part in the struggle Karyakin wrote about, was not even called to the plenary although he was a so-called candidate member of the Central Committee.

The months that followed were marked by silence about Solzhenitsyn. The attention of the Party and the new leadership was focused on the political reconstruction, the quiet purges and changes of officials after the removal of Khrushchev. A certain degree of political relaxation was noticeable in the nation. For a very short time the atmosphere even gave hope of a limited, balanced cultural liberalization or at least, a "normalization" in the spirit of "reality"—a slogan used by the new collective leadership in the beginning. Was the time of "hammer criticism" over, to be followed by an epoch of true and honest criticism? In Moscow, many intellectuals consequently attributed great significance to the publication of two contributions by Aleksandr Solzhenitsyn in the Soviet press at the end of 1965 and the beginning of 1966. The first (in *Literaturnaya Gazeta* on November 4) was a strongly polemical linguistic article, the other (in the January edition of *Novy Mir,* 1966) was the short story *Zakhar-Kalita.* Both these prose works showed a completely new aspect of Aleksandr Solzhenitsyn as a writer with a great feeling for the historical, linguistic and cultural —that is, *patriotic*—values of the Soviet Union.

Thus, it seemed in January as if both parties to the conflict were now willing to demonstrate some good faith: Solzhenitsyn by "writing in the patriotic theme", his foremost opponent—the leadership of *Literaturnaya Gazeta*—by giving him space in their columns, and *Novy Mir* by presenting him as an author with broader aspects than just the Stalin era—an interest that had characterized, at least according to his opponents, his writings so far.

But in reality, the struggle against Solzhenitsyn began at that very moment to take a different and more dangerous shape. It had grown into an affair for the state security service, KGB. It soon became clear that the KGB was collecting evidence against him. A slanderous campaign of unclear origin was started. Solzhenitsyn however, turned out to be an unusually stubborn and fearless opponent. Thanks to his earlier familiarity with methods of provocation, his evidently extensive knowledge of people, his intelligence and fearlessness, he managed to escape the traps that were constantly set for him.

He developed a technique that turned sly as well as overt official accusations against him into dangerous boomerangs.

The Invisible Front

Solzhenitsyn's friends soon noticed that the secret police was taking a keen interest in the author. "The Invisible Front" was using its entire arsenal of grotesque weapons including surveillance, wire-tapping and censorship of mail.

In 1964 Solzhenitsyn sent three copies of *The First Circle* to *Novy Mir*. The magazine accepted the manuscript without much deliberation. In September of 1965, however, the author requested the copies to be returned to him for some minor corrections.

Since the novel was voluminous he deposited the copies temporarily with a good friend—Teush, the mathematician—in Moscow.

Four days later, the KGB searched Teush's apartment. They confiscated the copies of *The First Circle,* the play *Feast of the Conquerors* (a poetic drama which Solzhenitsyn had written "in his head" in the camp of Ekibastuz but had never intended to publish) and his personal literary archives. Later, in the campaign against Solzhenitsyn reports were circulated that the manuscripts seized from Teush had been found by Customs Officials in the possession of a "tourist" whose name was never revealed.

Solzhenitsyn immediately protested to the Central Committee. Meanwhile, Teush was being interrogated by the Secret Police. The protest did not have any effect, and it became more and more obvious that people connected with the KGB were using the confiscated material in an attempt to place Solzhenitsyn in a compromising situation, perhaps to tie him to the 'smuggling' of the manuscripts. This probably explains why Soviet agents like Victor Louis were busy "smuggling" out the manuscripts of *Cancer Ward* and *The First Circle,* as well as material from the confiscated literary archives, until the Zurich lawyer Heeb appeared in the picture. On the other hand a "genuine" smuggling of manuscripts was evidently going on at the same time through different channels—most of Solzhenitsyn's prose was already circulating in copies (*samizdat*) passed from reader to reader in the Soviet Union. Some of these versions reached publishers in the West. One consequence of this traffic was a dispute over the copy-right of *Cancer Ward*.

Louis and Pavel Licko, who both brought out copies of this novel to the West, also published interviews with Solzhenitsyn. They first gave the impression of being pro-Solzhenitsyn but their interviews contained statements and implications that could easily be manipulated and used against the author, which in fact, was done later. An example was the statement claiming that Solzhenitsyn never believed himself innocent of the "crimes" for which he was sentenced in 1945. That statement originated from Licko. Victor Louis was the source of the impression of Solzhenitsyn as a talented writer but a dreadful man. The opinion of Solzhenitsyn as a writer with a martyr-complex was also initiated by Victor Louis.

In the spring and summer of 1965 it became obvious that the KGB was not only interested in Solzhenitsyn but also in his supporters. The author himself and several of his closest friends including Lev Kopelev and the famous gerontologist Zhorez Medvedev, were put under close surveillance and were even shadowed. One reason for this was apparently the fact that the KGB wanted to chart Solzhenitsyn's relationship with the so-called intellectual opposition and particularly, with those involved in the distribution of *samizdat* publications—officially, illegal literary works (and political pamphlets) that had not been approved by the censorship bureau or had been banned by the agency. So, in 1964 his *Prose Poems* which had been circulated as *samizdat* copies reached the Russian emigrant magazine *Grani* in West Germany where they were published. These were soon to be followed by the rest of Solzhenitsyn's prose works, one after another.

"The Reshetovskaya Case"

In early 1965 Solzhenitsyn and Natalya Reshetovskaya were planning to move out of Riazan where they had been living ever since the rehabilitation.

Solzhenitsyn had been encountering great difficulties at Riazan ever since the publication of *One Day in the Life of Ivan Denisovich*. He was regarded as a particularly controversial person in his hometown, especially because of his book *The Good of the Cause*, which in fact gives a very detailed description of a true case—a legal scandal which had occurred in Riazan. For all this the local Party stalwarts gathered against him. As a result of this controversy he was put under "total surveillance" by the local Secret Service. The authorities refused to give him assistance to get a better apartment. Zhorez Medvedev recounts in his book about Soviet science policy that Solzhenitsyn was living "in a damp, wooden house without any conveniences".

Solzhenitsyn did not have the right to move to Moscow as he was refused permission to register as a resident there. Both he and his wife were attracted by the science center in Obninsk, so in January 1965 Natalya Reshetovskaya applied for a job as an assistant professor at the Scientific Research Institute there—a position for which she had been recommended by the Scientific Council of the Institute which had voted massively in her favour.

According to Zhorez Medvedev, who disclosed the scandal, Natalya Reshetovskaya was undoubtedly the most qualified of all the candidates. In addition to being an outstanding researcher, she was a competent teacher, which was a vital advantage for this office. Her specialities were Physical Chemistry and Biochemistry.

However, after having been recommended by the Scientific Council, the problem of arranging an apartment for her arose. It was then that it was revealed that she was married to the controversial writer Aleksandr Solzhenitsyn. Some Party officials at Obninsk panicked and alerted the central authorities in Moscow.

Weeks of strange manipulation passed by. Solzhenitsyn mentioned the scandal in a discussion with the head of the Ideological Commission of the Central Committee, Pyotr Demichev. It was possible that he had then not been informed of what was going on—the intrigues might have been carried on at a lower level. In any case, Demichev, as a result of the conversation, promised to intervene against what he did not hesitate to call "legal violations" in the Reshetovskaya case.

In the presence of Solzhenitsyn he called up the head of the Party of the Kaluga district which Obninsk belonged to, ordering him to facilitate their moving to Obninsk.

But Demichev did not keep his promise. Prominent members of the Presidium of the Academy of Medical Science took action to prevent Reshetovskaya from getting this position at Obninsk. They invalidated the decision of the Scientific Council and even went as far as changing the membership of the council, supposedly after a vote they had taken.

After a series of peculiar manipulations at the highest possible level by their enemies the Solzhenitsyns were prevented from moving to Obninsk.

The situation was mysteriously complicated in another way. One of those who were actively trying to get Reshetovskaya appointed was the internationally famous geneticist Nikolai Vladimirovich Timofeyev-Resovsky, head of the Department of Radiobiology and Genetics at the Obninsk Institute. For many years he had been harassed by Trofim Lysenko, the dictator in the field of Biology and related branches of science during Stalin's era.

Timofeyev-Resovsky had to pay a high price for his conflict with Lysenko. Shortly after the end of the war he was accused of being a Chilean spy and arrested. As mentioned before, he spent several months in a cell in the Butyrki prison in Moscow together with Solzhenitsyn.

After that Timofeyev-Resovsky was sent to different labor camps and also had to work in a "sharashka".

Timofeyev-Resovsky's background and relationship with Solzhenitsyn and Reshetovskaya *almost* resulted in a scientific "Pasternak affair". In December 1965, he was rewarded with a prestigious American prize for his findings in the field of genetics. However, no one in the Board of the Soviet Academy of Sciences had ever heard of this award as it had never before been given to scientists outside the United States. Colleagues who apparently were motivated by sheer envy tried to persuade Timofeyev-Resovsky to turn down the prize which, they claimed, had been given to him for provocative purposes. However, Timofeyev-Resovsky refused to do so, and before further pressure could be brought to bear on him the insignias were delivered in an almost coup-like fashion by a visiting vice-president of the American Academy of Arts and Sciences.

The 23rd Party Congress

The 23rd Party Congress in Moscow, held from March 29 to April 8, 1966, turned into some kind of official watershed. It marked the ultimate end of the "thaw" under Khrushchev and heralded the hopes of the intellectuals for a liberalization. Tvardovsky who had played such an important part at the previous congress in 1961, was not even a delegate; so it was evident to everybody from the beginning that he would not be re-elected as a "candidate member" of the Central Committee. His own publication, *Novy Mir,* became the target of frequent attacks at the congress. Instead of Tvardovsky the Nobel laureate Mikhail Sholokhov was permitted to appear as the spokesman for Soviet intellectuals. His speech came close to a prosecutor's plea in a treason trial—a prosecutor who even gave vent to his dissatisfaction with the "gentleness" of Soviet law.

In the fall of 1965, the authors Andrei Sinyavsky and Yuri Daniel were arrested on charges of smuggling anti-Soviet manuscripts to the West. Sinyavsky was sentenced to seven years imprisonment with hard labor and Daniel, to five. The trial resulted in widespread and continuous protests and unrest among the intellectuals which consequently led to a confusing tangle of new arrests and purges within the artists' unions and organizations.

The crackdown on the rebellious intellectuals received a great deal of attention at the Party Congress. Many speakers mentioned this problem either directly or indirectly. There were no personal attacks against Aleksandr Solzhenitsyn but many references seemed to have been hewn for him and the kind of literature he represented.

Leonid Brezhnev, the Party-leader, emphasized in his report to the Congress on March 29 that the Party "will lead an uncompromising struggle against all appearances of ideologies irrelevant to us". He went on to state that " 'craftsmen' who have specialized in defaming and slandering our system instead of serving our heroic People are, unfortunately, to be found among us. Self-evidently these people are isolated cases. They do not in any way express the feelings and thoughts of our creative intelligentsia. These apostates do not even respect the most sacred cause of the Soviet citizen: the interests of our Socialist Fatherland. It is very understandable, that the Soviet People cannot silently overlook the shameful activity of these people. The People treat them according to their merits."

The following day the Party secretary in Moscow, Yegorytchev, spoke much in the same vein:

"It has become fashionable lately to look for elements of so-called 'Stalinism' in the nation's political life, with the purpose of frightening the public, especially the intelligentsia. We are saying: gentlemen, that you won't succeed! No one will succeed in defaming the front troops of the international Communist movement! . . . . The Party also decisively rejects all attempts to wipe out the heroic History of our People . . . ."

Associating with Brezhnev's report, the Belorussian Party-leader Pyotr Masherov declared:

"It is surprising how hurriedly and easily unimaginative and artistically weak works—occasionally even directly harmful ones—are being published both in the pages of popular magazines and separately. Nevertheless, these magazines and publishing houses are led by Communists. Where are their Party principles and their responsibility to the Party and the People?"

Similar accusations were levied by the Party secretary, Konotop, of the Moscow district. He criticised the magazines *Novy Mir* and *Yunost* in addition to certain films and stage plays which "sometimes give a distorted picture of our Soviet life by revelling in single deficiencies and difficulties, developing skepticism and lack of political consciousness and by intentionally picturing the leaders as opponents of the collectives.

Publishers of magazines and books printing ideologically harmful works are, in fact, whether they want to admit it or not, rejecting the principles of literature created in adherence to the spirit of the Party and the People."

The rudest appearance, however, was made by Mikhail Sholokhov who presented himself as a good example of how a true Communist patriot should behave abroad. He castigated Sinyavsky and Daniel, characterizing both as traitors and misfits who would not have escaped execution during the Revolution. But first of all Sholokhov addressed himself to those who had been defending the "apostates":

"I am not ashamed of those who have been slandering the Fatherland and soiling what is dearest to us. They are immoral. I am ashamed of those who have been trying and are still trying to defend them . . . . What we have fought for has cost us too much, and the Soviet State is too valuable to us to be slandered and defamed unpunished . . . ."

Cancer Ward is "Approved"

All this time Aleksandr Solzhenitsyn had not yet been mentioned by name publicly. It was evident that it had been decided that he should be made a "non-person" in the Orwellian sense; his name was excluded by the censors from all literary articles and literary encyclopedias. *One Day in the Life of Ivan Denisovich* was removed from the shelves of many libraries in the country, but this was more as a result of the apprehension of the librarians and not because they had received direct orders from the Authorities. Solzhenitsyn later revealed that at this time he was banned from appearing publicly. Thus, in November, 1966, nine out of eleven scheduled appearances were cancelled at the last minute, and not even the reading of his works on the radio was allowed. Material he had sent to different magazines and publishers were either turned down or put aside.

Meanwhile however, Solzhenitsyn's supporters became more active. On November 17, 1966, a large number of the members of the Prose Section of Moscow's Writers' Union gathered to discuss the first part of *Cancer Ward*. The session was presided over by Georgi Beriozko. Solzhenitsyn must have experienced this as a rather unexpected triumph—many prominent writers and critics unmistakably sided with him. The atmosphere at this meeting was so favorable to Solzhenitsyn that his sworn opponents were forced to restrain themselves to only very modified and well concealed criticism. The following is a strictly condensed summary of viewpoints expressed at the meeting.

Georgi Beriozko. I am very happy that our first meeting about a piece of work of considerable talent will be based only on facts. This is a debate on a novel which is not yet completed. I do hope it will be fruitful.

Aleksandr Borshchagovsky. I am sure that *Cancer Ward* will be published . . . . The first part of it is so important and, to my opinion, so pleasant and so necessary that we hardly expect to be confronted with another work of such urgency in the near future . . . a work of the same penetration as [Leo Tolstoy's] *The Death of Ivan Ilyich* and on the same level as [Saltykov-Shchedrin's] *Golovlev Family* . . . *Cancer Ward* is an outstanding novel which will obviously get to the printing press and add to our understanding of life. It also brings us closer to the borders without which our society is unable to progress.

Venyamin Kaverin. Solzhenitsyn's entire work is characteristic of our time. The new fashion of writing is here and the old literature coiling like a snake has come to an end . . . Solzhenitsyn is a writer of great significance. It is up to him whether he will be a great author or not. . . . It is hard to judge an unfinished work but even now it can be said that this is a book of tremendous honesty . . . . Why has the manuscript not been printed yet? Do they still exist, those who were defending the Rusanov terror? The new way of writing is a bridge between the fifties and the sixties. All attempts to silence Solzhenitsyn are doomed to fail. He cannot write differently.

I. Vinnichenko. I believe that it is of no use calling Solzhenitsyn a great man. However, he is undoubtedly a prominent writer . . . . He is a writer who is physically unable to distort truth . . . . I do not agree with those who find the manuscript full of pessimism and lack of faith in science . . . . This is a true work of art revealing a malignant tumor in our society.

Nikolai Asanov. It is essential that the book is published, with our assistance.

A. Mednikov. In due course the critics will realize why he has reached his present position in literature and in the minds of the public . . . . If Solzhenitsyn had not existed, someone else inevitably, would have said the same thing.

Lev Slavin. Already, at this stage, the novel appears to be one of the most powerful and most vital works in recent years.

Zoya Kedrina (People started to leave during her appearance). Undoubtedly a talented and mature writer . . . a very interesting piece of work, and I do not doubt it will be printed. However, it needs a lot of work . . . so that the writer's ideas and attitudes to social questions will be emphasized more.

L. Kabo. The impact of the manuscript is fantastic. It is self-evident it will become a book.

V. Sarnov. Kedrina and Asanov persist in giving Solzhenitsyn instructions . . . . When I was reading *One Day in the Life of Ivan Denisovich* I had a feeling of joy and happiness that great Literature was back. I would not think of *Cancer Ward* as being of the same quality as *One Day* . . . I wish Aleksandr Isaevich many more years of life, but I also wish that all his works would be published in his lifetime . . . .

Yuri Karyakin. It is obvious to all of us that *Cancer Ward* must be published. I want to give political—not pseudo-political— reasons for that. Rusanov is not a danger of the past. Men like him are still alive dreaming of their time to come . . . .

Yelisar Maltsev. I want to see Solzhenitsyn's manuscript in print. I experienced a fantastic feeling of joy and solemnity when reading it, and I am happy I have had the opportunity of getting to know the writer.

R. Sazhin. I cannot get rid of my doubts as to whether we really have any right to give the writer advice. The only right we have is to say that the novel is a great success.

Yelena Tager. A remarkable work of art indeed . . . . Solzhenitsyn stands on the level of the great tradition and his talent will not be wasted.

Grigori Baklanov. In the Army I got used to the fact that when an officer of a higher rank was asking for advice, it did not necessarily mean that he really wanted to listen. It seems to me as if some speakers today have been misusing their right to give Private Solzhenitsyn some advice . . . . It is scandalous that the novel has not yet been published.

A. Belinkov. The voice of great literature . . . . Like other great artists, the writer, Solzhenitsyn, has succeeded in revealing still another new aspect, so far unknown to us, of a historical period. The literary work of Solzhenitsyn does not only resemble the Renaissance; his work in fact is a renaissance of Russian spiritual life. He has achieved something that is only possible for a man of true talent and genuine courage. That is the essence of Aleksandr Solzhenitsyn's work.

Only on major points did Solzhenitsyn not accept any of the

"officers' criticism" expressed at the meeting, including that by Zoya Kedrina. Solzhenitsyn disclosed in his address that there had been a controversy over the title of the novel, *Cancer Ward,* between himself and *Novy Mir.* He had been the loser of that fight; *Novy Mir* had turned down *Cancer Ward.* Therefore, he had sent the manuscript to a couple of other publications, *Zvezda* and *Prostor,* but had never received an answer from either of them.

Summarizing the discussion, Beriozko, the chairman of the meeting, stated that it would be of great value if "an important writer like Solzhenitsyn" would get more involved in "certain matters" (meaning ideology). However, Beriozko concluded the debate by saying that *Cancer Ward* "makes an overwhelming impression; it is a unique, artistically powerful achievement. To a certain extent, however, those who have pointed out the weaknesses in the character of Rusanov are right . . ."

The important result of the meeting was that the members, obviously unanimously, adopted a resolution stating that *Cancer Ward* should be published and that a report of the meeting be sent to the publications *Zvezda* and *Prostor.* (This was actually done and it was this very report that later reached the West.)

After the discussion O. Voitinskaya stood up demanding the publication of the novel by the organization's own periodical *Moscow.* Voitinskaya ended with an appeal to the Writers' Union of Moscow to "participate actively in the struggle for *Cancer Ward*".

An incident at the end of the meeting shows how heated the debate must have been despite the calm tone. The young poet Bella Akhmadulina (Yevtushenko's first wife) jumped onto the podium where Aleksandr Solzhenitsyn was sitting, shouting to him:

"You're a fantastic, man! Let us pray to God for Aleksandr Solzhenitsyn's health!"

The Fourth Congress of
Soviet Writers

On May 22, 1967, the Fourth Congress of Soviet Writers which had been postponed several times, finally convened. It had at least one ambition: to demonstrate a unity and balance that had not been achieved. Missing from the long list of 514 delegates were many writers who had been prominent in the cultural debate of the fifties and sixties, notably: Vladimir Dudintsev, Aleksandr Solzhenitsyn, Yevgeni Yevtushenko, Bulat Okudzhava, Yuri Kazakov, Boris Slutsky and Bella Akhmadulina.

The delegate Ilya Ehrenburg preferred to be out of town during the Congress—a fact which Mikhail Sholokhov was to be sarcastic about. Sholokhov frequently mounted the rostrum to scorn those who were demanding greater artistic freedom. He went as far as to declare that their spiritual fathers were the American Intelligence Agency (CIA), Stalin's daughter Svetlana Allilujeva and some Russian counter-revolutionaries.

Almost a whole year passed before the stenographic transcript from the Congress was published. The Congress as well as the protocol succeeded in turning Solzhenitsyn into a "nonexistent" person. His name was not mentioned even once in the ensuing so-called debate nor in the reports that were loaded with names of the latest "successes" in Russian prose literature since the previous Congress. His open letter to the Congress —which was the main topic of conversation behind the scenes and which was probably the only document of this congress for historians to remember, perhaps with the only exception of Sholokhov's extreme cynicism—was not even considered worth registering as a document related to the Congress. Nor did the Congress register the many manifestations of loyalty expressed in letters and telegrams addressed to the Congress Presidium by delegates and members of the Union of Soviet Writers.

Aleksandr Solzhenitsyn's letter of May 16, 1967

To the Presidium and the delegates to the Congress, to members of the Union of Soviet Writers, and to the editors of literary newspapers and magazines:
Not having access to the podium at this Congress, I ask that the Congress discuss:
1. The increasingly intolerable oppression, in the form of censorship, that our literature has endured for decades, and that the Union of Writers can no longer accept.
Under the obfuscating label of Glavlit, this censorship—which is not provided for in the Constitution and is therefore illegal, and which is nowhere publicly labeled as such—imposes a yoke on our literature and gives people unversed in literature arbitrary control over writers. A survival of the Middle Ages, this censorship has managed, like the old Methuselah, to stretch its existence almost to the twenty-first century. Of fleeting significance, it attempts to arrogate to itself the role of unfleeting time—that of separating good books from bad.
Our writers are not supposed to have the right, are not endowed with the right, to express their considered judgment about the moral life of man and society, or to explain in their own way the social problems and historical experience that have been so deeply felt in our country. Works that might express the mature thinking of the people, that might have a timely and salutary influence in the realm of the human spirit or on the development of a social conscience, are proscribed or distorted by censorship on the basis of considerations that are petty, egotistical, and—from the national point of view—shortsighted. Outstanding manuscripts by young authors, as yet entirely unknown, are nowadays rejected by editors solely on the ground that they "will not pass" with the public. Many members of the Writers' Union, and even many of the delegates to this Congress, know how they themselves have bowed to the pressures

of the censorship and made concessions in the structure and
concept of their books—changing chapters, pages, paragraphs,
or sentences, giving them innocuous titles—just for the sake
of seeing them finally in print, even if it meant distorting them
irremediably. It is an understood quality of literature that gifted
works suffer most disastrously from all these distortions, while
untalented works are not affected by them. Indeed, it is the best
of our literature that is published in mutilated form.

Meanwhile, the most censorious labels—"ideologically harmful," "depraved" and so forth—are proving short-lived and
fluid, in fact are changing before our very eyes. Even Dostoevsky, the pride of world literature, was at one time not published in the Soviet Union (up to now his works are not published in full); he was reviled and excluded from the school
curriculum made unavailable for reading. For how many years
was Yesenin not considered "counter revolutionary"?—he was
even subjected to a prison term because of his books. Wasn't
Mayakovsky called "an anarchistic political hooligan"? For
decades the immortal poetry of Akhmatova was considered
anti-Soviet. The first timid printing of the dazzling Tsvetaeva
ten years ago was declared a "gross political error". Only after
a delay of twenty to thirty years were Bunin, Bulgakov, and
Platonov returned to us. Inevitably Mandelshtam, Voloshin,
Gumilev, and Kliuev will follow in that line—not to mention
the recognition, at some time or other, of even Zamyatin and
Remisov.

A decisive moment in this process comes with the death of
a troublesome writer. Sooner or later after that, he is returned
to us with an "explanation of his errors". For a long time the
name Pasternak could not be pronounced aloud; but then he
died, and since then his books have appeared and his verse is
even quoted at official ceremonies.

Pushkin's words are really coming true: "They are capable
of loving only the dead".

But the belated publication of books and rehabilitation of
names does not make up for either the social or the artistic
losses suffered by our people as a consequence of these monstrous delays and the suppression of artistic conscience. (In
fact, there were writers in the nineteen-twenties—Pilnyak,
Platonov, Mandelshtam—who called attention at a very early
stage to the beginnings of the personality cult and to the pe-

culiar traits of Stalin's character; but these writers were silenced and destroyed instead of being listened to.) Literature cannot develop in between the categories of "permitted" and "not permitted", "about this you may write" and "about this you may not". Literature that is not the breath of contemporary society, that dares not transmit the pains and fears of that society, that does not warn in time against threatening moral and social dangers—such literature does not deserve the name of literature— it is only a facade—it loses the confidence of its own people, and its published works are used as wastepaper instead of being read.

Our literature has lost the leading role it played at the end of the last century and the beginning of this one, and it has lost the brilliance of experimentation that distinguished it in the nineteen-twenties. To the entire world the literary life of our country now appears immeasurably more colorless, trivial, and inferior than it actually is or would have been if it were not confined and hemmed in. The losers are both our country—in world public opinion—and world literature itself. If the world had access to all the uninhibited fruits of our literature, if it were enriched by our own spiritual experience, the whole artistic evolution of the world would move along in a different way, acquiring a new stability and attaining even a new artistic threshold.

I propose that the Congress of Soviet Writers adopt a resolution which would demand and ensure the abolition of all censorship, open or disguised, of all fictional writing, and which would release publishing houses from the obligation to obtain authorization for the publication of every printed page.

2. The duties of the Union toward its members.

These duties are not clearly formulated in the statutes of the Union of Soviet Writers (under "Protection of copyrights" and "Measures for the protection of other rights of writers"), and it is sad to learn that for a third of a century the Union has not defended either the "other" rights or even the copyrights of persecuted writers.

Many writers have been subjected during their lifetime to abuse and slander in the press and from the rostrums of congresses and conferences, without being afforded the physical possibility of replying. More than that, they have been exposed to suppression and personal persecution—Bulgakov, Akhmatova, Tsvetaeva, Pasternak, Zoshchenko, Platonov, Alexander

Grin, Vasily Grossman. The Union of Writers not only did not make its own periodicals available to these writers for purposes of reply and justification, not only did not come out in their defense, but also, through its leadership, was always first among the persecutors. Names that adorned our poetry of the twentieth century found themselves on the list of those expelled from the Union or not even admitted to it in the first place. The leadership of the Union cravenly abandoned to their distress those for whom persecution ended in exile, labor camps, and death— Pavel Vasilev, Mandelshtam, Artem Vesely, Pilnyak, Babel, Tabidze, Zabolotsky, and others. The list must be cut off at "and others". We learned after the 20th Party Congress that there were more than six hundred writers whom the Union had obediently handed over to their fate in prisons and camps. However, the roll is even longer, and its curled-up end cannot and will never be read by our eyes. It contains the names of young writers and poets who we may have known accidentally through personal encounters, whose talents were crushed in the camps before being able to blossom, whose writings never got further than the offices of the State Security Service in the days of Yagoda, Yezhov, Beria and Abakumov.

There is no historical necessity for the newly elected leadership of the Union to share with its predecessors the responsibility for the past.

I propose that all guarantees for the defense of Union members subjected to slander and unjust persecution be clearly formulated in Paragraph 22 of the Union statutes, so that past violations of legality will not be repeated.

If the Congress does not remain indifferent to what I have said, I also ask that it consider the interdictions and persecutions to which I myself have been subjected.

1) It will soon be two years since the State Security authorities took away from me the manuscript of my novel, *The First Circle,* thus preventing it from being submitted to publishers. Instead, in my own lifetime, against my will and even without my knowledge, this novel has been "published" in an unnatural, "restricted" edition for reading by an unidentified select circle. My novel has thus become available to literary officicials but is being concealed from most writers. I have been unable to obtain open discussion of the novel within writers' associations or to prevent misuse and plagiarism.

2) Together with this novel, my literary papers dating back

fifteen to twenty years—material that was not intended for publication—was taken away from me by the State Police. Now, tendentious excerpts from these papers have also been covertly "published" and are being circulated within the same circles. The play, *Feast of the Conquerors,* which I wrote in verse in my mind in camp—where I was known by a three-digit number and where, condemned to die of starvation, we were forgotten by society, no one outside the camps rising against such repression—this play, the work of the remote past, is being ascribed to me as my very latest work.

3) For three years now, an irresponsible campaign of slander has been conducted against me, a man who fought all through the war as a Battery Commander and received military decorations. It is being said that I served time as a criminal, or that I surrendered to the enemy (I was never a prisoner-of-war), or again, that I "betrayed" my country and "served the Germans". This is the interpretation now being put on the eleven years I spent in camps and in exile for having criticized Stalin. This slander is being spread at secret meetings and conferences, by people holding official positions. I vainly tried to stop the slander by appealing to the Board of the Writers' Union of the RSFSR and to the press. The Board did not even react, and not a single newspaper printed my replies to the slanderers. On the contrary, slander against me from rostrums has intensified and become more vicious within the last year, making use of distorted material from my confiscated papers, but I have no way of replying.

4) My novel, *Cancer Ward,* the first part of which was approved for publication by the prose department of the Moscow Writers' Organization, cannot be published either by chapters or in its entirety.

5) The play, *The Love-Girl and the Innocent,* accepted in 1962 by the Sovremennik Theater, has thus far not been approved for performance.

6) The screen play, *The Tanks Know the Truth,* the stage play, *The Light That Is in You,* a group of short stories entitled *The Right Hand,* the series of *Prose Poems*—all these cannot find either a producer or a publisher.

7) My stories published in *Novy Mir* have never been printed in book form, having been rejected everywhere—by the Soviet Writer-Publishers, the State Literature Publishing House, and

the Ogonyok Library. They thus remain inaccessible to the general reading public.

8) I have also been prevented from having any contacts with readers either through public reading of my works (in November 1966, nine out of eleven scheduled meetings were cancelled at the last moment) or through reading over the radio. Even the simple act of giving a manuscript away for "reading and copying" has now become a criminal act—ancient Russian scribes were permitted to do this five centuries ago!

Thus, my work has finally been smothered, gagged, and slandered.

In view of such flagrant infringements of my copyright and "other" rights, will the Fourth Congress defend me? Yes, or no? It seems to me that the choice is not without importance for the literary future of several of the delegates.

I am of course confident that I will fulfill my duty as a writer under all circumstances—even more successfully and more unchallenged from the grave than in my lifetime. No one can bar the road to truth, and to advance its cause I am prepared to accept even death. But may it come about that repeated examples will finally teach us not to stop the writer's pen during his lifetime.

At no time has this ennobled our history.

Aleksandr Solzhenitsyn

The letter, which Solzhenitsyn distributed to hundreds of writers, received an extremely powerful response even if it was not commented on by the speakers at the Congress and was not even mentioned in the protocol. About one hundred writers including many prominent influential personalities, publicly supported Solzhenitsyn's pamphlet.

As a result 80 members of the Union of Soviet Writers sent a collective statement to the Congress Presidium. Some ten of them were delegates to the Congress. Among the 80 names were Konstantin Paustovsky, Venyamin Kaverin, Vladimir Tendryakov, Grigori Baklanov, Vladimir Soloukhin, Fazil Iskander, Boris Balter, Vasily Aksyonov, Yunna Morits, Bulat Okudzhava, Arseni Tarkovsky, Boris Slutsky and Vasil Bykov. The Congress delegate Valentin Katayev declared in a telegram that he was "fully sympathetic" to the main points in Solzhenit-syn's letter.

Letters written in the same spirit were sent to the Congress Presidium by Sergei Antonov, David Dar and Viktor Konetsky, who was a member of the Board of the Writers' Organization in Leningrad. In addition to these a long, frank letter on the principles of censorship was sent to the Congress Presidium by Georgi Vladimov, while the distinguished old poet, Pavel Antokolsky, wrote to the Party Secretary, Pyotr Demichev, who was directly responsible for cultural policy.

Solzhenitsyn's letter, dated May 16, reached several ad-dressees well in time for the opening of the Congress in the Kremlin Palace of Congresses on May 22. The meeting lasted five days. Throughout the proceedings—the protocol of which filled over 300 closely typed pages—the letter was totally ig-nored although it was the general subject of conversation in the lobbies of the Congress Hall and in the entire Western world. At the Congress the Swedish delegate Artur Lundkvist made a statement to some Swedish journalists which drew great attention. He insinuated that Solzhenitsyn's letter was queru-lous, adding that he had been assured that Solzhenitsyn's con-fiscated manuscripts would be returned to the owner and that an anthology of his short stories would be published as a book. Lundkvist's statement did not only spread to the Scandinavian press; it also reached Solzhenitsyn who, later, when forced to comment on it, disclosed that the reports were deliberately cir-culated lies. The rumors were probably spread in order to neu-tralize, as far as possible, the excitement caused by the letter or, as Solzhenitsyn put it, "to muffle public opinion." The letter, however, made the literary officials realize that it was not possible to reduce Solzhenitsyn to silence or to ignore some of the problems he had exposed.

On June 12, Solzhenitsyn met with four of the "heavyweight" secretaries of the Writers' Union: Georgi Markov, Konstantin Voronkov, Sergei Sartakov and Leonid Sobolev. Solzhenitsyn then brought up the issue of the slander campaign against him in his capacity of writer and war veteran. The officials declared that they saw it as their duty to answer the lies publicly, and promised "at least to look into the question" of the publication of *Cancer Ward*. The anthology was obviously not mentioned. *Cancer Ward* had been ready for a year, it having been completed in the summer of 1966. The Prose Section in Moscow had, as early as November 17 the same year, unanimously expressed itself in favor of the publication of the first part of the novel. At the time of Solzhenitsyn's meeting with the secretaries, the situation was very strange—the novel was neither banned nor allowed. For some time however, it had been circulated illegally as typewritten "samizdat". At the meeting of June 12, Solzhenitsyn therefore made the secretaries aware of the risk that the novel could be smuggled abroad illegally and published in an unauthorized version.

The summer passed without any new developments. On September 12, exactly three months after the discussion at the Secretariat, Solzhenitsyn sent a new protest letter addressed to all 42 secretaries of the Writers' Union. In this new letter Solzhenitsyn stated that his letter to the Congress had been supported by more than one hundred writers but had not even been answered. "Instead," to quote him, "homogenous, obviously centrally controlled rumors have been spread to calm public opinion that the archives and the novel have been returned to me, that *Cancer Ward* and a collection of short stories are in the process of being printed. As everybody knows these are all lies."

Referring to his discussion with the secretaries who, on June 12, promised to denounce the slander against him, Solzhenitsyn wrote:

"No such action has taken place; on the contrary the slander continues. At closed instruction meetings, activist gatherings and seminars, 'fresh, fantastic nonsense is spread about me—like the rumor that I have escaped to Egypt or England. I would like to assure my slanderers that it is more likely that they, rather than I, will escape. Prominent persons are very persistently expressing their regrets that I did not die in the camp but was released instead. Similar regrets were also heard shortly after the publication of *Ivan Denisovich*. This book is secretly being removed from the libraries."

Solzhenitsyn wrote also that the magazine *Novy Mir* was at last prepared to publish *Cancer Ward,* but that the permission had still not been granted.

He disclosed that *Cancer Ward* was already circulating in hundreds of typewritten "samizdat" copies. He indicated, furthermore, that the publication of the book abroad appeared imminent, and that it would obviously be the fault of the Writers' Union if that happened.

On September 22, thirty of the Union's forty-two secretaries gathered in the Writers' Club on Voronsky Street to discuss Solzhenitsyn's letter. This stormy meeting which lasted more than five hours, was also attended by the author himself and an official of the Cultural Sector of the Central Committee identified only as Melentiev. The chairman of the meeting was Konstantin Fedin, First Secretary of the Writers' Union. Below is a resumé of the statements, which were mostly formulated as accusations.

Konstantin Fedin. I was shaken by Solzhenitsyn's second letter. I sensed in it something in the nature of a threat. The second letter continues in the line of the first; but the first letter spoke more concretely and with more fervor about the fate of the writer, while the second, I feel, was offensive. None of us denies that he is talented. Yet the tenor of the letter veers in an impermissible direction. His letter is like a slap in the face to us—as if we were dullards and not representatives of the creative intelligentsia. In the final analysis, he himself is slowing down the examination of the subject of his demands.

Aleksandr Solzhenitsyn. It has become known to me that, in preparation for the discussion of *Cancer Ward,* the secretaries of the Board were instructed to read the play, *Feast of the Conquerors,* which I myself have long since renounced; I have not even read it for ten years. I destroyed all copies of it except the one that was confiscated and that has now been reproduced. More than once I have explained that this play was written not by Solzhenitsyn, member of the Union of Writers, but by a nameless prisoner, Sh-232, in those distant years when there was no return to freedom for political prisoners, and at a time when no one in the community, including the writers' community, either in word or in deed, spoke out against repression, even when such repression was directed against entire peoples. I now bear just as little responsibility for this play as many other authors bear for speeches and books they wrote in 1949 but would not write again today. This play bears the stamp of the desperation of the concentration camp in those years when a man's whole conscious being was determined by his social being, and at a time when the conscious being was by no means up-lifted by prayers for those who were persecuted. This play bears no relationship whatsoever to my present work, and the critique of it is a deliberate departure from a business-like discussion of the novel, *Cancer Ward*.

Moreover, it is beneath a writer's ethics to discuss a work that was seized in such a way from a private apartment. The critique of my novel, *The First Circle,* is again a separate matter and should not be substituted for a critique of the novel, *Cancer Ward*.

Aleksandr Korneichuk. I have a question to put to Solzhenitsyn. How does he regard the licentious bourgeois propaganda that his first letter evoked? Why doesn't he dissociate himself from the propaganda? Why does he put up with it in silence? How is it that his letter was broadcast over the radio in the West even before the Congress of Soviet Writers started?

Sergei Baruzdin. Even though Solzhenitsyn protests against the discussion of *Feast of the Conquerors,* we shall have to discuss this play whether he wants to or not.

Afanasi Salynsky. I would like Solzhenitsyn to tell us by whom, when, and under what circumstances these papers were removed. Has the author asked for their return? To whom did he address his request?

Solzhenitsyn. Very well, I shall answer these questions. It is not true that the letter was broadcast over the radio in the West before the Congress: it was broadcast *after* the Congress closed, and even then, not right away. Very significant and expressive use is made here of the word "abroad", as if it referred to some higher authority whose opinion was very much cherished. Perhaps this is understandable to those who spend much creative time traveling abroad, and to those who flood our literature with sketches about life abroad. But all this is alien to me. I have never been abroad, but I do know that I don't have time enough left in my life to learn about life there. I do not understand how one can be so sensitive to opinion abroad and not to opinion in one's own country—to pulsing public opinion here. During my entire life I have had the soil of my homeland under my feet; only *its* pain do I hear, only about *it* do I write.

Why was the play, *Feast of the Conquerors,* mentioned in the letter to the Congress? This can be seen from the letter itself: in order to protest against the illegal "publication" and dissemination of this play against the will of the author and without his consent.

Now, concerning the confiscation of my novel and papers. Yes, I did write several times, beginning in 1965, to protest this matter to the Central Committee of the Communist Party. But in recent days a whole new version of the confiscation of my archives has been invented. The story is that Teush, the person who was keeping my manuscripts, had some tie with another person who is not named, that the latter was arrested while going through customs (where, is not mentioned), and that something or other was found in his possession (they do not say what); it was not something of mine, but they decided to protect me against such an acquaintanceship. All this is a lie. Teush's friend was investigated two years ago, but no such accusation was made against him. The items I had in safekeeping were discovered as a consequence of police surveillance, wire-tapping, and eavesdropping. And here is the remarkable thing: hardly does the new version of the confiscation appear than it crops up in various parts of the country. Lecturer Potemkin has just aired it to a large assemblage in Riga; and one of the secretaries of the Union of Writers has passed it on to writers in Moscow, adding his own invention, namely, that I supposedly acknowledged all these things at the last meeting of the Secretariat. Yet, not a single one of these things was discussed.

Voice. Has the Editorial Board of *Novy Mir* rejected or accepted the novel, *Cancer Ward?*

Toktobolot Abdumomunov. What kind of authorization does *Novy Mir* require to print a story, and from whom does it come?

Aleksandr Tvardovsky. Generally, the decision to print or not to print a particular thing is a matter for the Editorial Board to decide. But in the situation that has developed around this author's name, the Secretariat of the Union must decide.

Konstantin Voronkov. Not once has Solzhenitsyn appealed directly to the Secretariat of the Union of Writers. After Solzhenitsyn's letter to the Congress, some of the comrades in the Secretariat expressed the desire to meet him, to answer questions, to talk with him and help. But after the letter appeared in the dirty bourgeois press and Solzhenitsyn did not react in any way . . .

Tvardovsky [interrupting]. Nor did the Union of Writers!

Voronkov. . . . this desire died. And now the second letter has come. It is written in the form of an ultimatum; it is offensive and a disrespect to our writers' community. Just now Solzhenitsyn referred to "one of the secretaries" who addressed a Party meeting of Moscow writers. I was that secretary. [To Solzhenitsyn] People hastened to inform you but they did a bad job of it. As to the confiscation of your things, the only thing I mentioned was that you had admitted at the last meeting that the confiscated items were yours and there had been no search made of your house. Naturally, after your letter to the Congress, we ourselves wanted to read all your works. But you should not be so rude to your brothers in labor and writing! And you, Aleksandr Trifonovich [Tvardovsky], if you consider it necessary to print *Cancer Ward,* and if the author accepts your correction, then go ahead and print it yourself. Why should the Secretariat be involved?

Tvardovsky. And what happened in the case of [Aleksandr] Bek? The Secretariat was also involved then and made its recommendations, but all the same nothing was published.

Voronkov. What interests me most of all now is the civic image of Citizen Solzhenitsyn: Why doesn't he answer the malicious bourgeois propaganda? And why does he treat us as he does?

Gabit Musrepov. I have a question, too. How can he possibly write in his letter: "Prominent persons persistently express regret that I did not die in the camp." What right does he have to write such a thing?

Adi Sharipov. And by what channels could the letter have reached the West?

Solzhenitsyn. Lots of things have been said about me. A person who right now occupies a very high position publicly declared that he is sorry he was not one of the "troika" that sentenced me in 1945, that he would have sentenced me to be shot there and then! Here, at the Secretariat, my second letter is interpreted as an ultimatum: either print the story or it will be printed in the West. But it isn't I who present this ultimatum to the Secretariat. It is life that presents this ultimatum to both you and me. I write that I am disturbed by the distribution of the story in hundreds—in hundreds of typewritten copies.

My works are disseminated in one way only: people persistently ask to read them, and having received them to read, they either use their spare time or their own funds to copy them and then give them to others to read. As long as a year ago the entire Moscow section of the Writers' Union read the first part of *Cancer Ward,* and I am surprised that Comrade Voronkov said here that they didn't know where to get it and that they asked the KGB. About three years ago my *Prose Poems* were disseminated just as rapidly: as soon as I gave the manuscript to people to read it quickly reached various cities in the Union. And then the editors of *Novy Mir* received a letter from the West from which we learned that these writings had already been published there. It was in order that such a fate might not befall *Cancer Ward* that I wrote my insistent letter to the Secretariat. I am no less astonished that the Secretariat could fail to react in some way to my letter to the Congress before the West did. And how could it fail to respond to all the slander that surrounds me? Comrade Voronkov has used the remarkable expression "brothers in writing and labor". Well, the fact of the matter is that these brothers in writing and labor have for two and a half years calmly watched me being hounded, persecuted, and slandered.

Tvardovsky. Not everyone has been indifferent.

Solzhenitsyn. . . . and newspaper editors, also like brothers, contribute to the web of falsehood that is woven around me by not publishing my denials. I'm not speaking about the fact that people in the concentration camps are not allowed to read my book, *One Day in the Life of Ivan Denisovich.* It was banned in the camps; searches were made and people were put in solitary confinement for reading it, even during those months when all the newspapers were loudly acclaiming it and promising that "this kind of thing will not happen again". But in recent times the book has been secretly withdrawn from libraries outside the camps as well. I have received letters from various places telling me of the prohibition against circulating the book. The orders are that readers should be told that the book is in the bindery, or that it is out, or that there is no access to the shelves where the book is kept, and to refuse to circulate it. Here is a letter recently received from Krasnogvardeisky Region in the Crimea:

"In the regional library, I was confidentially told (I am an activist in this library) of an order that your books be removed from circulation. One of the women workers in the library wanted to present me with *One Day* in a newspaper edition as a souvenir, since the library no longer needs it, but another woman immediately stopped her rash friend: 'What are you doing, you mustn't! Once the book has been assigned to the Special Section, it is dangerous to make a present of it.' "

I am not saying that the book has been removed from *all* libraries; here and there it can still be found. But people who had come to visit me in Riazan were unable to get my book in the Riazan Oblast Reading Room! They were given various excuses but they did not get the book . . . .

The circle of lies becomes ever wider, having no limits; they are even charging me with having been taken prisoner during the war and having collaborated with the Germans. But that's not the end of it! This summer, in the political education schools, for example, in Bolshevo, the Party propagandists were told that I had fled to the United Arab Republic and that I had changed my citizenship. Naturally, all this was written down in the propagandists' notebooks and is disseminated one hundred times over. And this took place no more than a few miles from the capital!

Here is another version. In Solikamsk, a certain Major Shestakov declared that I had fled to England, having taken advantage of a tourist visa. This man is the deputy for political affairs in his Army unit—who would dare to disbelieve him? Another time, the same man stated that I had been officially *forbidden* to write. Well, here at least, he is closer to the truth.

And from the rostrums this is what is being said about me: "He was set free prematurely, for no reason." Whether there was any reason can be seen in the court decision of the Military Collegium of the Supreme Court, Rehabilitation Section. This document has been presented to the Secretariat . . . . *Tvardovsky.* It also contains the combat record of Officer Solzhenitsyn.

Solzhenitsyn. And the expression "prematurely", isn't it really something? After having served the eight-year sentence, I was kept an additional month in prison, but of course, it is considered shameful even to mention such a petty detail. I spent three years in exile with that eternal feeling of doom. It was only thanks to the 20th Party Congress that I was set free—and this is called "prematurely"! The expression is so reminiscent of the conditions which prevailed in the 1949–53 period: if a man did not die beside a camp rubbish heap, if he was able even to crawl out of the camp, this meant he had been set free "prematurely"—after all, the sentence was for eternity and anything earlier was "premature".

Former Minister Semichastny, who was fond of speaking on literary issues, also singled me out for attention more than once. One of his astonishing, even comical, accusations was the following: "Solzhenitsyn is materially supporting the capitalist world; else why doesn't he collect his royalties from the publishers of his well-known book?"

Obviously, the reference was to *Ivan Denisovich,* since no other book of mine had been published at that time. Now, if you knew, if you had read somewhere that Comrade Semichastny felt that it was absolutely necessary for me to wrest the money from the capitalists, then why didn't you inform me about it? This is a farce; whoever collects royalties from the West has sold out to the capitalists; whoever does not take the money is materially supporting them. And the third alternative?—To go to heaven. While Semichastny is no longer a minister, his idea has not died. The All-Union Society for the Dissemination of Scientific Information has carried it further. The idea was repeated on July 16 of this year by Lecturer A. A. Freifeld at the Sverdlovsk Circus. Two thousand persons sat there and marveled: "What a crafty bird, that Solzhenitsyn! Without leaving the Soviet Union, without a single kopeck in his pocket, he contrived to support world capitalism materially." This is indeed a story to be told at a circus.

We had a talk on June 12, right here, at the Secretariat. It was quiet and peaceful. We seemed to make some progress. A short time passed, and suddenly rumors spread all over Moscow. Everything that actually took place was distorted, beginning with the fabrication that Tvardovsky had been shouting and waving his fist at me. But everyone who was there knows that nothing like that took place. Why these lies, then? And right now we are all hearing what is said here, but where is the guarantee that after today's meeting of the Secretariat everything will not be distorted again? If you really are "brothers in labor and writing", then my first request is that when you talk about today's session, don't fabricate and distort things.

I am one person; my slanderers number hundreds. Naturally I am never able to defend myself, and I never know against whom I should defend myself. I wouldn't be surprised if I were declared to be an adherent of the geocentric cosmic system and to have been the first to light the pyre of Giordano Bruno.

Salynsky. I shall speak of *Cancer Ward.* I believe that it should be printed—it is a vivid and powerful work. To be sure, it contains descriptions of diseases in pathological terms, and the reader involuntarily develops a phobia about cancer—a phobia which is already widespread in our century. Somehow I think this aspect of the book should be eliminated. The caustic, topical-satirical style should also be eliminated. Another negative feature is that the destinies of almost all the characters are connected with the concentration camp or with camp life in one form or another. This may be all right in the case of Kostoglotov or Rusanov, but why does it have to be applied to Vadim, to Shulubin, and even to the soldier? At the very end we learn that he is no ordinary soldier from the Army, that he is a camp guard. Still, the basic orientation of the novel is to discuss the end of the difficult era of our past.

And now a few words about moral Socialism, a concept expounded in the novel. In my opinion, there is nothing bad about this. It would be bad if Solzhenitsyn were preaching *amoral* Socialism. If he were preaching national Socialism or the Chinese version of national Socialism it would have been bad. Each person is free to form his own ideas of Socialism and its development. I personally believe that Socialism is determined by economic laws. But of course, there is room for argument. Why not print the story then?

Konstantin Simonov. I do not accept the novel, *The First Circle,* and oppose its publication. As for *Cancer Ward,* I am in favor of having it published. Not everything in the story is to my liking, but it does not have to please everyone. Perhaps, the author should take into account some of the comments that have been made, but naturally he cannot adopt all of the suggestions. It is also our duty to refute the slander about him. Furthermore, his book of stories should be published. The foreword to the latter would be a good place in which to publish his biography, and in this way the slander would die by itself. Both we and he himself can, and must, put an end to false accusations. I have not read *Feast of the Conquerors,* nor do I desire to do so, since the author doesn't wish it.

Tvardovsky. Solzhenitsyn's position is such that he cannot issue a statement. It is we ourselves, the Union, who must make a statement refuting the slander. At the same time, we must sternly warn Solzhenitsyn against the inadmissible and unpleasant way in which he addressed the Congress. The Editorial Board of *Novy Mir* sees no reason why *Cancer Ward* should not be printed, naturally, after certain revisions. We only wish to receive the Secretariat's approval or at least word that the Secretariat does not object.

[He asks Voronkov to produce the Secretariat's draft communiqué which was prepared in June. Voronkov indicates that he is in no hurry to produce the communiqué. During this time, exchanges are heard: "They still haven't decided. There are those who are opposed!"]

Fedin. No, that isn't so. It isn't the Secretariat that has to print or reject anything. Are we really guilty of anything? Is it possible, Aleksandr Trifonovich, that you feel guilty?

Tvardovsky [quickly, expressively]: I? No.

Fedin. We shouldn't search for some trumped-up excuse to make a statement. Mere existence of the rumors does not provide sufficient grounds for doing so. It would be another matter if Solzhenitsyn himself were to find a way to resolve the situation. What is needed is a public statement by Solzhenitsyn himself. But think it over, Aleksandr Isaevich—whose interest will be served by our publishing your protests? You must protest above all against the dirty use of your name by our enemies in the West. Naturally, in the process, you will also have the opportunity to vent some of the complaints you've uttered here today. If this proves to be a fortunate and tactful document, we will print it and help you. It is precisely from this point that your justification must proceed, and not from your works, or from this bartering as to how many months we are entitled to in examining your manuscript. Three months, four months, is that really so important? It is far more frightening that your works are used there, in the West, for the basest of purposes.

Korneichuk. We didn't invite you here to throw stones at you. We summoned you in order to help you out of this trying and ambiguous situation. You were asked questions but you declined to answer them. By our writings we are protecting the interests of our Government, our Party and our People. Here you have sarcastically referred to trips abroad as if they were pleasant strolls. We travel abroad to wage the struggle. We return home from abroad, worn out and exhausted, but with the feeling of having done our duty. Don't think that I was offended by the comment concerning travel sketches. I don't write them. I travel on the business of the World Peace Council. We know that you suffered a great deal, but you are not the only one. There were many other comrades in the camps besides you. Some were old Communists. From the camps they went to the front. Our past consists not of acts of injustice alone; there were also acts of heroism—but you didn't notice them. Your works consist only of accusations. *Feast of the Conquerors* is malicious, vile, offensive! And this foul play is disseminated, and the people read it! When were you imprisoned? Not in 1937. In 1937 *we* went through a great deal, but nothing stopped us! Konstantin Alexandrovich Fedin was right in saying that you must speak out publicly and strike out against Western propaganda. Do battle against the foes of our nation! Do you realize that thermonuclear weapons exist in the world and that despite all our peaceful efforts the United States may employ them? How then can we, Soviet writers, not be soldiers?

Solzhenitsyn. I have repeatedly declared that it is dishonest to discuss *Feast of the Conquerors,* and I demand that this argument be excluded from our discussion.

Alexei Surkov. You can't stop everyone from talking.

Vadim Kozhevnikov. The long time lapse between the receipt of Solzhenitsyn's letter and today's discussion is in fact an expression of the *seriousness* with which the Secretariat approaches the letter. If we had discussed it at the time, while the impact was still hot, we would have treated it more severely and less thoughtfully. We ourselves decided to find out just what kind of anti-Soviet manuscripts these were, and we spent a good deal of time reading them. The military service of Solzhenitsyn has been confirmed by relevant documents; yet we are not now discussing the officer but rather the writer. Today, for the first time, I have heard Solzhenitsyn renounce the libellous depiction of Soviet reality in *Feast of the Conquerors,* but I still cannot get over my first impression of this play. For me, this moment of Solzhenitsyn's renunciation of *Feast of the Conquerors* does not alter my perception of the play. Perhaps this is because in both *The First Circle* and *Cancer Ward* there is a feeling of the same vengeance for past suffering. And if it is a question of the fate of these works, the author should remember that he is indebted to the Party organ that discovered him. Some time ago, I was the first to express apprehension concerning *Matryona's House.* We spent time reading your gray manuscript, which you did not even venture to give to any Editorial Board. *Cancer Ward* evokes revulsion from the abundance of naturalism, from a surfeit of all manner of horrors. At the same time, its basic orientation is not medical, but rather social. . . . And it is apparently from this that the title of the work is derived. In your second letter, you demand the publication of your story, which still requires further work. Is such a demand worthy of a writer? All of our writers willingly listen to the opinions of the editors and do not hurry them.

Solzhenitsyn. Despite my explanations and objections, despite the utter senselessness of discussing a work written twenty years ago, in another era, in an incomparably different situation, by a different person—a work, moreover, which has never been published or read by anyone, and which was stolen from a drawer—some of the speakers have concentrated their attention on this very work. This is even more senseless than the action of the First Congress of Writers when it rebuked Maxim Gorky for *Untimely Thoughts* or Sergeyev-Tsensky for the *Osvagovskie Correspondence,* which had been published a good fifteen years earlier.

Vitali Ozerov. The letter to the Congress proved to be a politically irresponsible act. First of all, the letter reached our enemies. It contained things that were incorrect. Zamyatin was put in the same heap together with unjustly repressed writers. As regards the publication of *Cancer Ward,* we can make an agreement with *Novy Mir* that the book be printed only if the manuscript is corrected and the corrections are discussed. There remains some other very important work to be done. The story is uneven in quality. There are good and bad points in it. Most objectionable is the penchant for sloganeering and caricatures. I would ask that quite a number of things be deleted, things which we simply do not have time to discuss now. The philoso-

phy of moral Socialism does not belong merely to the hero.
One senses that it is being defended by the author. This cannot
be permitted.

Surkov. I have also read *Feast of the Conquerors.* The mood
of it is, "Be damned, the whole lot of you!" The same mood
pervades *Cancer Ward* as well. Having suffered so much, you
had a right to be angry as a human being, Aleksandr Isaevich,
but after all you are also a writer! I have known Communists
who were sent to camps, but this in no measure affected their
view of the world. No, your story does not approach fundamental problems in philosophical terms, but in political terms. And
then there is the reference to that idol in the Theater Square,
even though the monument to Marx had not been erected at
that time.

If *Cancer Ward* were to be published, it would be used
against us, and it would be more dangerous than Svetlana's
memoirs. Yes, of course, it would be good to forestall its publication in the West, but that is difficult. For example, in recent
times I have been close to Anna Andreyevna Akhmatova. I
know that she gave her poem "Requiem" to several people to
read. It was passed around for several weeks, and then suddenly
it was printed in the West. Of course, our readers are now so
developed and so sophisticated that no measly little book is
going to alienate them from Communism. All the same, the
works of Solzhenitsyn are more dangerous to us than those of
Pasternak: Pasternak was a man divorced from life, while Solzhenitsyn, with his animated, militant, ideological temperament,
is a man of principle.

Boris Riurikov. Solzhenitsyn has suffered from those who have
slandered him, but those who have heaped excessive praise on
him and have ascribed to him qualities that he does not possess
have also done him harm. If Solzhenitsyn is renouncing anything, then he should renounce the title of "standard-bearer of
Russian realism". The conduct of Marshal Rokossovsky and
General Gorbatov is more honest than that of his heroes. The
source of this writer's energy lies in bitterness and wrath. As
a human being, one can understand this. You write that your
works are prohibited, but not a single one of your novels has
been censored. I marvel that Tvardovsky asks permission from
us. I, for example, have never asked the Union of Writers for
permission to print or not to print.

Baruzdin. I happen to be one of those who, from the start, have not been captivated by the works of Solzhenitsyn. *Matryona's House* was already much weaker than his first work, *One Day in the Life of Ivan Denisovich.* And *The First Circle* is much weaker; so pitifully naive and primitive are the depictions of Stalin, Abakumov, and Poskrebyshev. But *Cancer Ward* is an anti-humanitarian work. The end of the story leads to the conclusion that "a different road should have been taken." Did Solzhenitsyn really believe that his letter "in place of a speech" would be read from the rostrum of the Congress? How many letters did the Congress receive?

Voronkov. About five hundred.

Baruzdin. Well! And would it really have been possible to get through them in a hurry? I do not agree with Riurikov: it is proper that the question of permission be placed before the Secretariat. Our Secretariat should more frequently play a creative role and should willingly advise editors.

Abdumomunov. It is a very good thing that Solzhenitsyn has found the courage to repudiate *Feast of the Conquerors.* He will also find the courage to think of ways of carrying out the proposal of Konstantin Alexandrovich Fedin. If we publish *Cancer Ward,* there will be more commotion and harm than there was from his first letter to the Congress.

Irakli Abashidze. I was able to read only 150 pages of *Cancer Ward* and therefore, can make no thorough-going assessment of it. Yet, I didn't get the impression that the novel should not be published. But I repeat, I can't make a thorough assessment. Perhaps the most important things are in the latter part of the book. . . . let Solzhenitsyn himself answer, perhaps first of all, for his own sake.

Petrus Brovka. In Belorussia there are also many people who were imprisoned. For example, Sergei Grakhovsky was in prison for twenty years. Yet he realized that it was not the People, not the Party, and not the Soviet Authorities that were responsible for illegal acts. The People have already seen through Svetlana's notes—that fishmonger twaddle—and are laughing at them. But before us stands a generally acknowledged talent, and therein lies the danger of publication. Yes, you feel the pain of your land, even to an extraordinary degree. But you don't feel its joys. *Cancer Ward* is too gloomy and should not be printed.

Kamil Yashen. The author is not tortured by injustice; he is rather poisoned by hatred. People are outraged that there is such a writer in the ranks of the Union of Writers. I would like to propose his expulsion from the Union. He is not the only one who suffered, but the others understand the tragedy of the time better. The hand of a master is discernible in *Cancer Ward.* The author knows the subject better than any physician or professor. As for the siege of Leningrad, he now blames "still others" besides Hitler. Whom? We don't know. Is it Beria? Or today's outstanding leaders? He should speak out plainly.

Berdi Kerbabaev. I read *Cancer Ward* with a feeling of great dissatisfaction. Everyone is a former prisoner, everything is gloomy, there is not a single word of warmth. It is downright nauseating to read. It is not enough that he has repudiated *Feast of the Conquerors.* I would consider it courageous if he repudiated *Cancer Ward.* Then I would embrace him like a brother.

Sharipov. I wouldn't make any allowances in his case—I'd expel him from the Union. In his play, not only is Suvorov presented negatively but also, everything Soviet. I completely agree: let him repudiate *Cancer Ward.*

Leonid Novichenko. In the ideological and political sense, moral Socialism is the negation of Marxism-Leninism . . . Rusanov is a disgusting type who is correctly described. But it is unacceptable, that he changes from being a type to the upholder and expression of our society.

Georgi Markov. We await a clear answer from Solzhenitsyn regarding the bourgeois slander; we await his statement in the press. He must defend his honor as a Soviet writer. What with the excellent collaboration that has been established between *Novy Mir* and Aleksandr Isaevich, this story can be finished, even though it requires very serious work. But of course, it would be impossible to put it into print today. All the same, I still consider him our comrade. But, Aleksandr Isaevich, it's your fault and no one else's that we find ourselves in this complicated situation. As to the suggestions concerning his expulsion from the Union, given the conditions of comradeship that are supposed to prevail, we should not be unduly hasty.

Solzhenitsyn. I have already spoken out against the discussion of *Feast of the Conquerors* several times today, but I shall have to do so again. In the final analysis, I can rebuke all of you for not being adherents of the theory of development if you seriously believe that in the span of twenty years and in the face of a complete change in all our circumstances, a man does not change. But I have heard an even more serious thing here: Korneichuk, Baruzdin, and someone else mentioned that the people are reading *Feast of the Conquerors,* as if this play were being disseminated. I shall now speak very slowly; let my every word be taken down accurately. If *Feast of the Conquerors* is being widely circulated or printed, I solemnly declare that the full responsibility lies with the organization which had the only remaining copy—one not read by anyone—and used it for "publication" of the play during my lifetime and against my will; it is this organization that is disseminating the play! For a year and a half I have repeatedly warned that this is very dangerous. I imagine that there is no reading room where one is handed the play to be taken home. For, at home, there are sons and daughters, and desk drawers are not always locked. I had already issued a warning before, and I am issuing it again today!

Now, as to *Cancer Ward,* I am being criticized for the very title of the story, which is said to deal, not with a medical case, but with some kind of symbol. I reply that this symbol is indeed harmful, if it can be perceived only by a person who had himself experienced cancer and all the stages of dying. The fact is that the subject is specifically and literally cancer—a subject avoided in literature, but nevertheless a reality as its victims know only too well from daily experience. These may include your relatives, or soon perhaps, someone among those present will be confined to a ward for cancer patients, and then he will understand what kind of a "symbol" it is.

I absolutely do not understand why *Cancer Ward* is accused of being anti-humanitarian. Quite the reverse is true: life conquers death, the past is conquered by the future. Were this not the case, I would not by my very nature have undertaken to write it. But I do not believe that it is the task of literature to conceal the truth, or to tone it down, with respect either to society or the individual. Rather, I believe that it is the task of literature to tell people the real truth as they expect it. Moreover, it is not the task of the writer to defend or criticize one or another mode of distributing the social product, or to defend or criticize one or another form of Government organization. The task of the writer is to select more universal and eternal questions—the secrets of the human heart and conscience, the confrontation of life with death, the triumph over spiritual sorrow, the laws of the history of mankind that were born in the depths of time immemorial and that will cease to exist only when the sun ceases to shine.

I am disturbed by the fact that some comrades simply did not read certain passages of the story attentively, and hence, formed the wrong impressions. For example, "twenty-nine weep and one laughs", was a popular concentration-camp saying addressed to the type of person who would try to go to the head of the queue in a mess-hall. Kostoglotov comes out with this saying only so that he may be recognized, that's all. And from this people draw the conclusion that the phrase is supposed to apply to the entire Soviet Union. . . . Surkov surprised me. At first I couldn't even understand why he was talking about Marx. Where does Marx come into my story? Alexei Aleksandrovich [Surkov], you are a poet, a man with sensitive taste, yet in this case your imagination played a trick on you. You didn't grasp the meaning of this scene. Shulubin cites Bacon's ideas and employs his terminology. He says "idols of the market", and Kostoglotov tries to imagine a marketplace and in the center, a gray idol; Shulubin says "idols of the theater", and Kostoglotov pictures an idol inside a theater—but that doesn't work, and so it must be an idol in a theater square. How could you imagine that this referred to Moscow and to the monument to Marx that had not yet even been built?

Comrade Surkov said that only a few weeks after Akhmatova's "Requiem" had been passed from hand to hand, it was published abroad. Well, *Cancer Ward* has been in circulation for more than a year. And this is what concerns me, and this is why I am hurrying the Secretariat.

One more piece of advice was given to me by Comrade Riurikov: to repudiate Russian realism. Placing my hand on my heart, I swear that I shall never do it.

Riurikov. I did not say that you should repudiate Russian realism, but rather that you should repudiate your role as it is interpreted in the West.

Solzhenitsyn. Now, concerning the suggestion of Konstantin Aleksandrovich [Fedin], well, of course, I do not welcome it. Publicity is precisely what I am relentlessly trying to attain. We have concealed things long enough—we have had enough of hiding our speeches and our manuscripts under seven locks. Now, we had a previous discussion of *Cancer Ward*. The Prose Section decided to send a transcript of the discussion to interested Editorial Boards. Some likelihood of that! They have hidden it; they barely agreed to give me, the author, a copy. As for today's transcript, Konstantin Aleksandrovich, may I hope to receive a copy?

Konstantin Aleksandrovich Fedin has asked: "What interest would be served should your protests be printed?" In my estimation, the answer is clear: the interest of Soviet literature. Yet, it's strange that Konstantin Alexandrovich says that I should resolve the situation. I am bound hand and foot, and my mouth is closed—how am I to resolve the situation? It seems to me that this would be an easier matter for the mighty Union of Writers. My every line is suppressed, while the entire press is in the hands of the Union. Still, I don't understand and don't see why my letter was not read at the Congress. Kostantin Aleksandrovich proposes that the fight we waged not against the causes but rather against the effects and against the furor of the West surrounding my letter. You wish me to print a refutation—of what, precisely? I can make no statement whatsoever concerning an unprinted letter. And, most important, my letter contains a general part and a personal part. Should I renounce the general part? Well, the fact is that I am still of the same mind as I was then, and I am not renouncing a single word. After all, what is the letter about?

Voices. Censorship!

Solzhenitsyn. You haven't understood anything if you think it is about censorship. This letter is about the destiny of our great literature, which once conquered and captivated the world but which has now lost its standing. In the West they say the Russian novel is dead, and we gesticulate and deliver speeches saying that it is not dead. But rather than make speeches we should publish novels—truly good novels. Thus, I have no intention of repudiating the general part of my letter. Should I then declare that the eight points in the personal part of my letter are unjust and false? But they are all just. Should I say that some of the wrongs I protested against have already been eliminated or corrected? But not one of them has been eliminated or corrected. What, then, can I declare? No, it is you who must clear at least a little path for such a statement: first, publish my letter, then issue the Union's communiqué concerning the letter, and then indicate what is being corrected. Then I will be able to make my statement, and will do so gladly. If you wish, you can also publish my statement of today concerning *Feast of the Conquerors,* though neither the discussion of a stolen play nor the refutation of unprinted letters makes any sense to me. On June 12, here at the Secretariat, I was assured that the communiqué would be printed unconditionally, and yet, today, conditions are posed. What has changed?

My book *Ivan Denisovich* is banned. New slanders continue to be directed at me. You can refute them, but I cannot. The only comfort I have is that I will never get a heart attack from this slander because I've been hardened in Stalinist camps.

Fedin. No, this is not the proper sequence. You must make the first public statement. Since you have received so many approving comments on your talent and style, you will find the proper form, you can do it. Your idea of our acting first has no sound basis.

Tvardovsky. And will the letter itself be published in this process?

Fedin. No, the letter should have been published right away. Now the foreign countries have beaten us to it, why should we publish it?

Solzhenitsyn. Better late than never. So nothing will change regarding my eight points?

Fedin. We'll see about that later.

Surkov. You should state whether you renounce your role of leader of the political opposition in our country—the role they ascribe to you in the West.

Solzhenitsyn. Alexei Aleksandrovich [Surkov], it really makes me sick to hear such a thing—and from you, of all people: an artist with words and a leader of the political opposition? How does that make sense?

Then several statements followed demanding of Solzhenitsyn to accept Fedin's proposal. Solzhenitsyn repeated that he was unable to appear first since the Soviet reader would have no idea what it was all about.

The Secretariat meeting made the already rather chaotic situation even more confusing. After the meeting the slander campaign against Solzhenitsyn was intensified. Now, even members of the Central Committee joined in it. In this spirit the editor of the Party organ *Pravda,* Mikhail Zimyanin, made a monstrous speech at the Press Club in Leningrad on October 5. He attacked three writers: Yevgeni Yevtushenko, Andrei Voznesensky and particularly, Aleksandr Solzhenitsyn.

Zimyanin aimed the most slanderous charges at Solzhenitsyn: that the writer had been a prisoner of war and might not have been innocent when he was sentenced, and furthermore, that he wanted to make a martyr of himself. Zimyanin further enriched the debate by claiming that Solzhenitsyn was mentally disturbed—more precisely, schizoid:

"Solzhenitsyn is presently playing a particularly big role in the propaganda of the capitalist nations. He, too, is a psychically abnormal person, a schizoid. He was a prisoner of war and had to meet with—justly or unjustly—reprisals. He expresses his bitterness against the regime in his works. The prison camp is the only subject in his books, and he is unable to reach outside its framework. This theme is an obsession. Solzhenitsyn's works are directed against the Soviet system. He is only looking for sores and cancer tumors in it. He does not notice any positive features in our society.

In my official capacity I also have to read unpublished works and I have recently read Solzhenitsyn's play *Feast of the Conquerors.* This play deals with reprisals against those who are returning from the front. It is very much an anti-Soviet work. In the past people used to be imprisoned for things like this.

It is understandable that we cannot publish his works. Solzhenitsyn's demands for publication of his works cannot therefore be met. Well, if he writes stories in the interest of our society, then he will be published. No one is going to take the bread out of his mouth. Solzhenitsyn is a teacher of physics; well, then he could teach. He is very fond of appearing in public and frequently reads his works to different audiences. This possibility he has. He considers himself an ingenious writer . . . ."

The Secretariat discussion of September 22 wound up with

an appeal, supported by the majority of the 30 attending secretaries, to Solzhenitsyn to denounce the way in which his name was being used abroad for "anti-Soviet purposes".

On November 25 Konstantin Voronkov, secretary of the Writers' Union reminded Solzhenitsyn of the appeal and demanded a reply. Aleksandr Solzhenitsyn delivered his answer on December 1, in the following terms:

"In your letter number 3142 of November 25, 1967 the following questions are unclear to me:

1) Does the Secretariat intend to defend me against the three year-long continuous (mildly called unfriendly) slander campaign against me in my native country? In this there have been some new facts. On October 5, 1967, Pravda's editor Zimyanin, at a frequented meeting at the Press Club in Leningrad, repeated the worn out lie that I had been a prisoner of war. He also used the experienced method, practiced against unwanted persons, of calling me schizoid, and my past in camps an obsession. Lecturers from the Party Committee of the city of Moscow have been presenting more false versions of my activities "in the Army", where they claim that I had formed what they sometimes called a "defeatist", and at other times a "terrorist" organization. It is unbelievable that The Military Collegium of the Supreme Court did not notice that.

2) What action has been taken by the Secretariat to lift the illegal ban on my printed works in the libraries and on the instructions given by the censorship agency to exclude my name from articles? (The publication *Voprosy Literatury* did that even in a translation of a Japanese article. Also, at the University of Perm sanctions were taken against a group of students who wanted to discuss my printed works in their scientific anthology.)

3) Does the Secretariat want to stop an uncontrolled publication of *Cancer Ward* abroad or is the Secretariat indifferent to this risk? Are any steps being taken to have excerpts of the story published in *Literaturnaya Gazeta,* and the entire story printed in *Novy Mir?*

4) Does the Secretariat not intend to recommend to the Gov-

ernment the need for our country to join the Universal Copyright Convention? Then our writers would have an appropriate instrument for protecting their works from being illegally published abroad and for ending the shameful hunt of commercial translations.

5) Has the distribution of the illegal "citation edition" of my archives finally been stopped in the six months that have passed since my letter to the Congress, and has this edition been destroyed?

6) What steps have been taken by the Secretariat to have my confiscated archives and the novel, *The First Circle*, returned to me—that is, putting aside the official statement by Secretary Ozerov that they have already been returned?

7) Has the Secretariat approved or turned down Konstantin Simonov's recommendation that an anthology of my stories should be published?

8) Why haven't I yet received the stenographic transcript of the Secretariat meeting of September 22, so that I would be able to study it?"

In a very long letter to Konstantin Fedin in mid-January of 1968 Aleksandr Tvardovsky was able to disclose that *Cancer Ward* was already circulating by the "thousands" in the Soviet Union and that at any time, it would be published in France and Italy. Tvardovsky disclosed that the first eight chapters of the book had been set to type and that he had planned to publish them in the January issue of *Novy Mir,* but that the publication was stopped.

In this situation Tvardovsky demanded that excerpts of *Cancer Ward* be published immediately in *Literaturnaya Gazeta* with the note: "to be published in full in *Novy Mir*". He also required that the publishing house Sovetsky Pisatel be instructed to come out with an anthology of short stories including a biography of Solzhenitsyn; the biography that was supposed to stop the slander campaign was, according to Tvardovsky, also to be printed by either of the publications of the Writers' Union: *Literaturnaya Gazeta* or *Literaturnaya Rossiya.*

Tvardovsky further revealed that while he was writing the

long letter, dated January 7–15, he had received a telephone call from his publisher Goslitizdat who was publishing his complete works, that the fifth volume was underway. One of the articles in the volume was on the Jewish poet Samuil Marshak and carried a reference on Aleksandr Solzhenitsyn, probably in connection with the controversy about the Lenin Prize. Goslitizdat now demanded that Tvardovsky leave out Solzhenitsyn's name; the publishing house claimed that "instructions" had been received that Solzhenitsyn was not to be mentioned.

A similar disclosure regarding a ban on Solzhenitsyn's name was made by the writer Grigori Svirsky at a meeting with Moscow's writers' organizations on January 21–22. Svirsky made a violent and all-out attack against censorship; the only result of his appearance was that he was expelled from the Party and turned into a "non-person".

On January 25 Venyamin Kaverin sent a letter to Konstantin Fedin, his close friend since childhood. Kaverin was trying, as Tvardovsky had done, to persuade Fedin to revoke his decision to ban the publication of *Cancer Ward*. He implied that both union secretaries, Georgi Markov and Konstantin Voronkov, had in fact spoken in favor of the publication while Fedin—with all his power, in his capacity as First Secretary of the Writers' Union—had been absolutely against it.

"It is possible", said Venyamin Kaverin in his letter, "that there are persons in the Board of the Writers' Union, who believe that they are punishing the writer by deporting him to the world of foreign literature. They are punishing him with world-wide fame which is being used by our opponents for political purposes".

Central Directives

In February and March ideological conferences were held in all Party districts throughout the Soviet Union. Members of the top leadership of the Party participated in many of these meetings. Thus, Leonid Brezhnev addressed the nation's largest Party organizations—those in Leningrad and Moscow. Premier Alexei Kosygin appeared in Minsk, Belorussia, Kiev, and Pyotr Shelest in the Ukraine.

Strangely enough, the speeches by the top leaders were only published in the local press. In Minsk, Kosygin launched a very bitter attack against anti-Soviet propaganda, particularly foreign broadcasts. The same theme—the impossibility of ideological coexistence—was repeated in most of the speeches throughout the nation. According to the published resolutions, the main thesis stated that the capitalist world had started a merciless ideological war against Solzhenitsyn and that the most refined methods were being used.

On April 9–10 the Soviet Central Committee convened, and later announced a decision which marked a new phase in Soviet domestic as well as foreign policy. The plenary session had obviously laid down the basis for the struggle against "revisionism" within and without the country, which was to characterize Soviet policy for many months ahead.

Following the plenary session in April the members of the Presidium, again as in February, set out on nationwide trips to explain the decisions to the local organizations. None of the many speeches at the plenary meeting were published; neither were the statements made by the Party leaders at the conferences afterward. During the second half of April, however, the provincial press published a series of like resolutions, in which the local Party organizations confirmed their support of the decisions and the way in which the leadership had handled the most urgent questions concerning world, as well as domestic policy, and ideological matters.

A freezing, cold wind blew around these documents and the accompanying editorials and press comments. The Central Committee's resolution of April 10 read:

"The present stage of the historical development is characterized by a violent sharpening of the ideological struggle between Capitalism and Socialism. The entire gigantic apparatus of anti-Communist propaganda is aimed at weakening the unity of the Socialist countries and the international Communist movement, shattering the progressive forces of our time and undermining the Socialist society internally . . . ."

The basis for this concept was obviously the contagious "revisionist" developments in Czechoslovakia and Poland, the strongly anti-Soviet Cultural Revolution in China, the Romanian moves toward independence, successful anti-Communist revolutions, such as those that occured in Ghana and Indonesia and also, the direct military confrontation between East and West in Vietnam and the situation in the Middle East.

The situation, as now presented, was that the Soviet Union, with its military strength, had forced the "imperialists" into a growing *ideological* warfare in which all resources were being invested with the purpose of weakening the Soviet Union and its allies from the *inside*.

The weapons of this ideological war consisted of broadcasts and psychological sabotage in the form of refined rumor and propaganda campaigns. The goal of the anti-Communist propaganda was now to create anxiety, sow seeds of doubt and undermine the morale and labor discipline of the Soviet People.

Commenting on the new thesis an editorial in *Pravda* on April 19 stated that the imperialists, above all, were supporting "nationalist and revisionist elements" in this growing ideological struggle.

After this, different Czechoslovak tendencies which, for some time, had been watched with a feeling of deep discomfort, began to be attacked openly in the Soviet Union. A similar anxiety was caused by the activities of students and writers in Poland. With the addition of the rebellion and growing frankness of individual Soviet intellectuals, the parallel to the situation in 1956 was too obvious. The continued development of the Solzhenitsyn affair must be seen against this background.

The War of the Agents

Toward the middle of April when it became evident that both *Cancer Ward* and *The First Circle* had been smuggled abroad, Solzhenitsyn's situation became critical. Hectic activity involving political as well as police agents developed around him and his works. The Secretariat of the Writers' Union, the KGB and Russian emigrant and propaganda organizations connected with the CIA, were active in this war of agents which met all the standards of James Bond in vulgarity and maliciousness.

On April 16, Solzhenitsyn sent a notice to the members of the Union of Soviet Writers, reminding them that almost a year had passed since he presented his questions to the Writers' Congress. Since then, he had on three occasions written to the Secretariat of the Writers' Union and paid personal visits there. But his questions remained unanswered. His situation had not changed in any respect. His confiscated literary works had not been returned, his books were not approved for publication, his name was not allowed to appear in print. He also revealed that the Secretariat had stopped the Prose Section of Moscow's writers organization from discussing the second part of *Cancer Ward.*

"A year has passed", wrote Solzhenitsyn, "and now it has inevitably happened: chapters of *Cancer Ward* were recently published in the Times Literary Supplement. Nor has further publication been stopped; it might be a question of inexact and incomplete versions. This development forces me to inform our literary organization by the enclosed letter and statements in order that the attitude and responsibility of the Writers' Union may be clarified."

Solzhenitsyn enclosed his letter of April 12, 1967, to the

Secretariat of the Writers' Union, statements received from the Secretariat conference ten days earlier, a short letter of February 25, 1967, from the union secretary, Konstantin Voronkov, and Solzhenitsyn's own letter to the Secretariat dated December 1 the same year.

Solzhenitsyn's intense action was tactically, rather unwise in this situation. The political leaders, particularly in Moscow, East Berlin and Warsaw, were at this moment busy, nervously trying to find a means of putting down the "revisionism" in Dubcek's Czechoslovakia. Solzhenitsyn's "ethical Socialism" showed too much resemblance to Dubcek's "Socialism with a human face" and "the manifesto of 200 words". Besides too many Czechoslovak cultural personalities and journalists had already demonstrated too much interest in Solzhenitsyn's "reformist" Socialism. The "Spirit of Spring" he represented reminded the leadership only too much of the 1956 rebellion among the authors in the Soviet Union, Poland and Hungary.

Only two days after this notice to members of the Writers' Union, Solzhenitsyn sent another letter, this time addressed to the Secretariat of the Union. He sent copies to the magazines *Novy Mir* and *Literaturnaya Gazeta* and also, to the members of the Union. This letter read:

"At the editorial offices of *Novy Mir* I was shown the following telegram:
IMO 177. Frankfurt-am-Main. Ch 2 9 16.20. Tvardovsky. *Novy Mir*. This is to inform you that the Committee of State Security, acting through Victor Louis, has sent one more copy of *Cancer Ward* to the West, in order thus to block its publication in *Novy Mir*. Accordingly we have decided to publish this work immediately. The editors of the journal *Grani*.
I would like to protest both against the publication of my work in *Grani* and against the action of V. Louis, but the turbid and provocative nature of the telegram requires, first of all, the clarification of the following:
1) Whether the telegram was actually sent by the editors of the journal *Grani* or whether it was sent by a fictitious person. (This can be established through the international telegraph

system; the Moscow telegraph office can wire Frankfurt-am-Main.)

2) Who is Victor Louis, what kind of person is he, of what country is he a citizen? Did he really take a copy of *Cancer Ward* out of the Soviet Union, to whom did he give it, and where else are they threatening to publish it? Furthermore, what does the Committee of State Security (KGB) have to do with this?

If the Secretriat of the Writers' Union is interested in establishing the truth and in stopping the threatened publication of *Cancer Ward* in Russian abroad, I believe that it will help to get prompt answers to these questions.

This episode compels us to reflect on the terrible and dark avenues by which the manuscripts of Soviet writers can reach the West. It constitutes a grim reminder to us that literature must not be brought to such a state that literary works become a profitable commodity for any scoundrel who happens to have a travel visa. The works of our authors must be printed in their own country and must not become the plunder of foreign publishing houses."

A couple of days later Aleksandr Solzhenitsyn received further information via foreign newspapers about what had happened to the copies of *Cancer Ward* that had been taken out of the Soviet Union through different channels, one of which obviously was "the KGB agent Victor Louis"—a Soviet journalist of French descent who, among other things, was involved in an attempt to prevent the publication of Svetlana Alliluyeva's *Twenty Letters to a Friend*. Louis also acted as a public relations agent for Valeri Tarsis at the time of his pseudo-defection to England, and he was probably involved in the publication of Nikita Khrushchev's memoirs in 1970.

On April 21 Aleksandr Solshenitsyn sent the following letter to *Literaturnaya Gazeta*, organ of the Writers' Union, to *Le Monde* and the Italian Communist newspaper, *Unità:*

"I have learned from a news story published in *Le Monde* on April 13, that extracts and parts of my novel, *Cancer Ward,* are being printed in various Western countries, and that the publishers—Mandadory (Italy) and The Bodley Head (England)—are already fighting over the copyright to this novel (since the USSR did not sign the Universal Copyright Convention) despite the fact that the author is still living!

I would like to state that no foreign publisher has received from me either the manuscript of this novel or permission to publish it. Thus, I do not recognize as legal, any publication of this novel without my authorization—at present or in the future—and I do not grant the copyright to anyone. I will prosecute any distortion of the text (which is inevitable in view of the uncontrolled duplication and circulation of the manuscript) as well as any unauthorized adaptation of the work for the cinema or theater.

I already know from my own experience that all the translations of *One Day in the Life of Ivan Denisovich* suffered because of the haste with which they were made. Evidently, the same fate awaits *Cancer Ward* as well. Besides the question of money, literature itself is involved here.

A. Solzhenitsyn."

Time was obviously running out. *Literaturnaya Gazeta,* however, did not rush things. It took the magazine of the Writers' Union over two months to publish Solzenitsyn's letter and when finally did appear it was accompanied by an ideological thunderstorm—a long editorial article.

Meanwhile, several things had happened. The letter to *Le Monde* was confiscated but not the one to *Unità,* which published in full on June 4. A little more than a month before that, on April 30, the editorial staff of the Russian emigrant publication *Grani,* which is published by the publisher Possev in Frankfurt-am-Main, had publicly announced that they had "for a considerable time" been in possession of a copy of *Cancer Ward. Grani* had refrained from publishing the novel since there were still hopes that it would be published in *Novy Mir.*

Toward the end of March, however, the First Secretary of the Soviet Communist Party, Leonid Brezhnev, in a speech to Party activists in Moscow, made it clear that works like *Cancer Ward* could not be published in the Soviet Union.

At approximately the same time the editorial staff of *Grani* had received the information that the KGB (the Soviet Security Service) had decided on committing "sabotage" by sending out an additional copy of *Cancer Ward* to the West. Consequently, *Grani,* on April 8, sent a telegram informing the editor of *Novy Mir,* Aleksandr Tvardovsky, that the KGB, through Victor Louis' action, was trying to hinder the publication of *Cancer Ward* in *Novy Mir.*

Grani then announced that "the most important chapters" of *Cancer Ward* would be published in the May issue, adding that it was known that several well-known West European publishing houses had managed to get hold of copies of *Cancer Ward.*

On June 26 *Literaturnaya Gazeta* published Solzhenitsyn's letter. This version, however, did not include the statement published in *Unità* that the unauthorized, distorted editions might hurt his name. It is not known whether this far from unimportant sentence had been dropped by Solzhenitsyn himself or by the magazine. The letter was accompanied by a long editorial article with the headline "The Struggle of Ideas: the Writer's Responsibility". There was no doubt about the purpose of the article: to neutralize the effect of Solzhenitsyn's dissociation from pirate editions of his works published by publishers and magazines in the West.

The article dealt with the controversies around Solzhenitsyn in the past years in such a way that a shadow of flagrancy and criminality was cast on him. Even his biography was questioned in a vile manner.

Referring to the Secretariat meeting of September 22, 1967 *Literaturnaya Gazeta* said that Solzhenitsyn was warned that his name was being exploited by "reactionary Western propaganda" with provocative, anti-Soviet purposes. But Solzhenitsyn had "remained deaf to this kind of warning" and had refused to clarify his position toward "the shameless tumult of which he had become a so-called hero". This accusation was however totally false since Solzhenitsyn on several occasions during, as well as after, the Secretariat meeting, had cautioned against what was going to happen in case his manuscripts were published in uncontrolled versions abroad. In fact, at this time hardly any problem worried Solzhenitsyn more than the consequences of the smuggling of his manuscripts.

The article portrayed Solzhenitsyn as a "multifaceted," shrewd man with an academic education in Physics and Mathematics who has been active as a teacher.

The biographical part of the article noted that Solzhenitsyn spent "the last years of the war as the Commander of an anti-aircraft battery" and that he had received military honors. In reality he was drafted during the first year of war, on October 18, 1914, and by no means was he serving at any "anti-aircraft battery", but at the advanced front artillery. By these distortions *Literaturnaya Gazeta* created the impression that Aleksandr Solzhenitsyn's performance in the war was rather poor and that he had hardly anything to do with personal courage. It is true that the article mentioned the fact that he received military honors but did not report which ones, probably because that would have changed the image—the Red Star and the Order of the Patriotic War were no ordinary lapel buttons.

"He was sentenced shortly before the end of the war, charged with anti-Soviet activities, and served his term in a prison camp. He was rehabilitated in 1957," continued *Literaturnaya Gazeta.*

The article was formulated in a specially vicious way. "Served his term" implied that Solzhenitsyn was in fact not innocent of the "anti-Soviet activities" for which he was sentenced in July 1945. He certainly was "rehabilitated," but as several persons, including Valentin Turchin, pointed out in protest letters to *Literaturnaya Gazeta,* the word "rehabilitation" in this context only meant "release".

A. Solzhenitsyn was accused of not having participated in the external activities of the Writers' Union (he had in fact never been asked to do so) but had instead preferred to "attack the fundamental principles guiding Soviet literature". According to the magazine he had also violated the statutes of the Writers' Union which he voluntarily pledged to observe when he joined

the organization. In this way, *Literaturnaya Gazeta* was implying that his expulsion from the Union was under serious consideration, although only a very small group of extremists had
indicated they were in favor of such an action at the Secretariat
meeting of September 22.

It was in this way that Solzhenitsyn's letter to the Secretariat
of the Writers' Congress was first mentioned by the Soviet press.
The letter had been sent to the Presidium as well as to "at least
250 other addresses"; Solzhenitsyn's action was said to have
violated "generally established rules of conduct". The Secretariat believed that behind this "misbehavior" lay the calcula-
tion that the letter would be copied and circulated, and that
it would become another "literary sensation". Solzhenitsyn's action, which so obviously was dictated by desperation, was now
interpreted as cheap sensationalism with the intention of creating publicity.

In the eyes of the Secretariat the letter, which "was easily
picked up by Western propaganda" resulted in "excessive anti-
Soviet tumult following Solzhenitsyn's statement that Soviet
literature was being suppressed. He has crossed out the victories
of this literature, which have been acknowledged by the whole
world".

Solzhenitsyn's demand for the Writers' Union to protect
members who are victims of slander and unjust persecution was
considered almost criminal: "such a paragraph would put the
Union's statutes above Soviet law which guarantees every Soviet
citizen equal protection against slander and unjust persecution".

The confiscation of Solzhenitsyn's archives and manuscripts
was also brought up in the article. *Literaturnaya Gazeta* quoted
the Public Prosecutor according to whom "no search has ever
been made of the home of Aleksandr Solzhenitsyn at Riazan"
and his "archives have not been confiscated." "What really
happened," *Literaturnaya Gazeta* continued quoting the Public
Prosecutor, "was that *anonymous, typewritten copies* of some
of Solzhenitsyn's manuscripts were discovered and confiscated
from a certain Teush *together with other compromising
material.*"

In this way the organ of the Writers' Union even managed to imply that Solzhenitsyn's literary archives covering a period of 15–20 years, the play *Feast of the Conquerors* and the novel *The First Circle* are "compromising material".

To emphasize the insinuation, the magazine explained that the Soviet Security Service (KGB) was able to trace Teush after the customs had discovered manuscripts containing "groundless slander" against the Soviet Union in the possession of a foreign tourist—whose name is not mentioned.

Literaturnaya Gazeta was thus in print, spreading the slander which so far, had been heard only "from the rostrums", and against which Solzhenitsyn had protested very strongly on many occasions.

In analyzing one of the confiscated manuscripts, *Feast of the Conquerors,* the magazine wrote that Solzhenitsyn, in this play, depicted the "Soviet Army as a crowd of blockheads, suppressors, marauders and vandals living only for their own private interests." The play was also considered sympathetic to the Vlasov troops (Vlasov was a Soviet general who defected to the Germans in the second World War) and to a certain Captain Nerzhin who helped a traitress to join Vlasov's army. This is undoubtedly an indirect accusation of treason against the writer; Nerzhin is Solzhenitsyn's *alter ego* in *The First Circle*.

The magazine admitted that Solzhenitsyn had protested against the fact that *Feast of the Conquerors* was described as his latest work. But then went on to ask: "how can one ignore the existence of this play when Solzhenitsyn, by entrusting his works to this distributor of anti-Soviet material abroad [Teush] loses control over them, including this play? How can one have objections against the fact that *Feast of the Conquerors* is being mentioned when one does not protest against the vital fact that Solzhenitsyn's name, literary works and letters to the Writers' Congress are being used by Western propaganda in the ideological struggle against the Soviet Union?"

Those who took part in the Secretriat meeting of September 22 had expected that Solzhenitsyn would have listened to their advice and dissociated himself from "the political provocations of Western propaganda". Solzhenitsyn's attitude however, had been characterized, as far as they were concerned, by "outspoken demagogy", and he had furthermore, "in an uncompromising tone", insisted that *Cancer Ward* be published immediately. *Cancer Ward* needed "thorough ideological rewriting", the magazine thought.

Solzhenitsyn was accused of having tried to make a deal with the Secretariat about concessions he would be willing to make in case *Cancer Ward* was published.

Konstantin Voronkov's letter of November 25, 1967, to Solzhenitsyn demanding that he clarify his position with regard to "the anti-Soviet uproar" was, according to *Literaturnaya Gazeta,* replied to in such a way that it seemed clear that Solzhenitsyn even in the future intended to use Western opinions as an instrument for putting pressure on the Writers' Union. The magazine thought also that Solzhenitsyn's April letter expressed a "pretended anxiety" over the forthcoming publication of *Cancer Ward* by "the most reactionary" publishers in the West, and that in his letters he "hypocritically" blamed the moral responsibility for the publication on the Secretariat of the Writers' Union.

Solzhenitsyn's report of the Secretariat meeting is called "tendentious and very subjective" and written with the purpose of creating the impression that the character and tone of the discussion had been favorable to himself.

Literaturnaya Gazeta also attacked Venyamin Kaverin's letter of defense to the First Secretary of the Writers' Union, Konstantin Fedin, declaring that the letter, in the same manner as Solzhenitsyn's account, "was distorting the attitude of some Secretariat members regarding the publication of *Cancer Ward*".

In reality Kaverin had written that the secretaries Georgi Markov and Konstantin Voronkov were ready to accept a decision of the Secretariat to publish the book while Fedin had been strongly opposed to that.

The magazine also tried to explain why it took Solzhenitsyn two months to get his note published in the Soviet Union. In this explanation the urgency of the note was totally minimized.

Solzhenitsyn was said to have written his letter in April when "excerpts of *Cancer Ward* were already being printed in the West" and when "a publication of the letter obviously had not changed anything".

Literaturnaya Gazeta criticized the factual contents of the letter by stating that in reality it only expressed concern for the possibility that the publishers, in their great hurry, might distort the text, but that Solzhenitsyn had not protested against the use of his name and works for anti-Soviet purposes.

The magazine literally demanded of Solzhenitsyn "a burning protest" against the actions of the foreign publishers and unwanted "protectors", and a declaration that he would not have anything to do with "*provocateurs* and enemies of the country." This was, however, not done by Solzhenitsyn, not even after several foreign publishing houses—"which continue to whip up anti-Soviet feelings"—had announced that they, too, intended to publish the novel, *The First Circle* which, according to *Literaturnaya Gazeta,* contains "vicious slander against our social system".

The magazine also claimed that it had become clear that Aleksandr Solzhenitsyn was completely satisfied with the role he had been given by the ideological opponents of the Soviet Union and was prepared only to protest in the same style as the protest just published. *Literaturnaya Gazeta* went on to say that Solzhenitsyn could use his literary skill to serve his Fatherland but instead, he was using it to the advantage of those who want to hurt his country.

The Pirate Editions

The pirate editions of *Cancer Ward* and *The First Circle* by the Western publishing houses made Aleksandr Solzhenitsyn internationally famous once more. After most of the excitement around *One Day in the Life of Ivan Denisovich* had died down Solzhenitsyn was a practically forgotten writer in the West. Between 1965 and 1968 no books by Solzhenitsyn were published in Western Europe or the United States. In most West European countries his works were not re-issued after 1963.

In 1968 *Cancer Ward* was published in Russian in Milan, Frankfurt-am-Main, London and Paris. It was followed, a few months later, by *The First Circle*, also in Russian, which was published in Frankfurt-am-Main, Belgrade, New York and London. The short story, *The Right Hand*, came out the same year in the Russian language in Frankfurt-am-Main and the play, *The Light That Is in You*, in London.

The copies of Solzhenitsyn's manuscripts which that year reached the Western publishers had arrived through different channels. The Soviet agent Victor Louis had obviously brought out copies of *Cancer Ward*, evidently trying to stop its publication in *Novy Mir*. It has also been suggested that the Slovak writer Pavel Licko who was active as a Soviet intelligence agent in World War II, played a similar role. Some copies of *Cancer Ward*, however, must have originated from a different source—most likely, the illegal "samizdat" publications in the Soviet Union. The same had obviously happened with *The First Circle*. The novel was printed in 1968 in two Russian versions, one, with the authentic title *V Kruge Pervom*, by the emigrant publishing house, Possev, in Belgrade, and the other by Harper & Row in New York. The same novel was published with the incorrect title *V Pervom Krugu* by Fischer Verlag in Frankfurt-am-Main and by the Romanian publisher Flegon in London. It was Flegon again who published the play, *The Light That Is in You.* Solzhenitsyn's Swiss lawyer prohibited the performance of this play in 1970, an action which affected the Swedish Broadcasting Corporation and some others.

In 1968 translations of *Cancer Ward* also appeared, in London, Neuwied, Berlin, Milan, New York, Helsinki, Paris, Stockholm and Rijeka (Yugoslavia), and of *The First Circle,* in London, Frankfurt-am-Main, Milan, New York and Paris.

With Solzhenitsyn's new international fame the desire of the authorities to pretend a coexistence, at least, with the writer came to an end.

The Fiftieth Anniversary

On December 11, 1968 Solzhenitsyn was celebrating his 50th birthday in Riazan. This fact was not mentioned by any Soviet newspaper. The following day the writer sent this short letter to *Literaturnaya Gazeta:*

"I know that your newspaper won't publish a single line by me without giving it a distorted and incorrect meaning. There is however, no other way for me to answer all the people who have sent me their congratulations.

I am deeply moved and want to thank those readers and writers who have sent me congratulations and wished me good luck on my 50th birthday. I promise them never to betray the truth. My only wish is that I will be worthy of the expectations of the Russian readers.

Riazan, December 12, 1968."

Literaturnaya Gazeta did not publish the letter.

An "Interview"

In the spring of 1969 some American newspapers, and later on the magazine *Survey,* printed an alleged interview with Solzhenitsyn by the Soviet journalist and agent, Victor Louis. The article was full of concealed accusations presented as "evidence". Louis claimed for example, that Solzhenitsyn knew very well that *Cancer Ward* and other works were being circulated as "samizdat" publications, but that he, "like any other Soviet citizen who has spent some time in a labor camp, is his own lawyer and knows the value of having an alibi".

Louis was thus implying that Solzhenitsyn himself saw to it that his works were illegally circulated, and in this way, smuggled abroad. Louis described the writer's methods in the following insinuating way:

"When writing letters, he knows that they eventually will find their way to Western newspapers, but he addresses them to members of the Union of Soviet Writers expecting one out of its hundreds of members to send them to the intended destination. Legally Solzhenitsyn cannot be charged with anything. Even if, like Tolstoy, he does not agree with the regime, he does not speak out frankly. He uses his dearly bought experience of the law so that no one can criticize him. It is difficult to charge him with having sent his novels abroad, but he is not at all surprised that they found their way there."

Using the same technique Victor Louis said that the next step Solzhenitsyn took was to protest against the publication of his books abroad, and did so "with admirable indignation" and even declared that he was going to sue the publishers.

"I don't know," Louis wrote, "whether he did so seriously believing that he could stop the printing the moment the protest reached the publisher who had bought one of these smuggled manuscripts, or whether he did it in plain naivity or as a calculated protest. He must have known that Pasternak too, protested in vain; but on the other hand, every writer has a natural wish to be published."

Louis added that Solzhenitsyn, unlike Sinyavsky or Daniel, could be accused of sending his manuscripts abroad; for, in any case, it could not be proved that he did not do so.

Very dubiously and without too much emphasis, Victor Louis then tried to deny the reports that he had smuggled out copies of *Cancer Ward*. In this interview, the authenticity of which has not been verified, Solzhenitsyn reportedly agreed that it had been meaningless to send an additional copy of the novel abroad since the magazine *Grani* already had one. "Besides", pleaded Louis, "if I am to be blamed for having sent out a copy, who sent the other ones? Why don't they share the blame with me?"

The reason, which Solzhenitsyn had mentioned earlier in his letter of protest, might have been that Louis (and Licko) unlike the other "smugglers" planned to prevent or block the publication of the novel in *Novy Mir;* for, the publication of it in the Soviet Union depended on whether or not it was published in the West.

Louis further claimed that Solzhenitsyn had refused to admit that he had accused him of irregularities "without having any evidence". Solzhenitsyn allegedly explained then that his letter to the Writers' Union had been based on "the provocative telegram" sent by the emigrant magazine *Grani* accusing Louis of smuggling the manuscripts out with the purpose of hindering their publication in the Soviet Union.

To make Solzhenitsyn look even more suspect Louis gave an account of some views expressed by Soviet authors, thereby taking the opportunity to spread the different allegations circulating in the domestic slander campaign against Solzhenitsyn. Thus, he introduced to the Western world the description (in the Soviet Union voiced by Pravda's editor Zimyanin and others at the Press Club in Leningrad) of Solzhenitsyn as a man with a martyr complex. They claimed that Solzhenitsyn was so deeply shaken by the time he spent in camps and deportation that he became almost incapable of staying away from this subject (the camps) in his works.

Another Soviet writer had reportedly told Victor Louis that since Solzhenitsyn is a talented writer "he was expected to produce something of permanent literary value—something without political dubiousness"—but this had not been done.

Still another author had allegedly said that he was under the impression that Solzhenitsyn was trying to say that the Russian peasants had known only two happy eras since the Revolution—that the first was during the period of the NEP (New Economic Policy) when minor private businesses were allowed and the collectivization of the farms had then not been accomplished; and the second was during the German occupation.

Louis finally accused Solzhenitsyn of not having protested against the publicity-oriented methods of the emigrant magazine *Grani,* saying that when such things were shown to Solzhenitsyn he simply refused to look at them so as not to reveal any personal reaction. He admitted that it was impossible, juridically, to accuse Solzhenitsyn of either agreeing or refusing to react—as long as he refused to read or listen to this kind of explanation. He observed further that Aleksandr Solzhenitsyn, although he did not agree with the Writers' Union on many points, did not want to return his membership card because it gave him considerable privileges and because it was the dream of every writer to belong to the Union. According to him the Union did not want to expel Solzhenitsyn because he was a popular writer who had been accepted as a member under unique circumstances.

The essence of "the interview", however seems to have been to explain to the Western world why Solzhenitsyn was going to become a "non-person" in his native country. Louis quoted an obviously false declaration allegedly made by Solzhenitsyn:

"I have ceased writing. Publicly. That's all. I have learnt my lesson."

In reality, the following year, Solzhenitsyn finished his novel about the Samsanov catastrophy in World War I, which he called: *August, 1914*. He had been writing on the subject periodically ever since 1937. Is it possible that he has written this voluminous novel only for his own pleasure, not for the public? The novel was offered to Soviet publishers in March 1971. In June it was published with Solzhenitsyn's authorization in Russian by YMCA-Press in Paris.

.

The Purge

The campaign against Tvardovsky's magazine, *Novy Mir* was intensified in the summer of 1969. A barrage of charges came from Ogonyok, and particularly, from the organ of the Writers' Union, *Literaturnaya Gazeta,* on August 27. The editorial leadership of *Novy Mir* was accused of having published many works that were later condemned by "the literary opinion". *Literaturnaya Gazeta* also demanded that those who had published "works that have been submitted to just criticism" be held responsible.

Toward the end of August, *Novy Mir* answered the attacks, but its defense no longer had any effect. *Novy Mir* had already surrendered most of its vital positions. At this point the attacks were decisive, fatal blows, obviously aimed at forcing Aleksandr Tvardovsky to resign as the editor and removing the other "liberals" from the editorial board. The political decision on Tvardovsky's removal and the purges within the Editorial Board of *Novy Mir* were probably approved in the late fall. Tvardovsky's resignation was formally announced in February, 1970, but even before this date he had effectively ceased to be editor of the magazine. By the removal of Tvardovsky, Solzhenitsyn lost his last possibility of getting his works published, and also, his foremost defender in the Soviet cultural hierarchy. The blow against *Novy Mir* and Tvardovsky and consequently, against Solzhenitsyn, was the very result of the so-called "April Plenary Session" which, in the spirit of the invasion of Czechoslovakia, announced an intensification of the struggle against foreign influence.

In 1969, some additional works by Solzhenitsyn reached the West. These included the short story, *The Easter Procession*

and the play, *The Love-Girl and the Innocent,* which had orig-
inally been accepted by the Sovremennik Theater in Moscow
at the end of 1962, but could not be staged because of an official ban. Other works that reached the West were *They Read
Ivan Denisovich* and *Answer to Three Students,* from the literary
archives confiscated by the KGB. In the Spring there were reports in the Soviet Union (which were published in the West)
of another great novel which, allegedly, had been smuggled
abroad. This novel, entitled *Archipelag Gulag* ("The Archipelago of the Prison Administration") was supposed to be the
last of a trilogy of which the first two were *Cancer Ward* and
The First Circle. The reports about this novel were very uncertain. There is no direct connection between *Cancer Ward* and
The First Circle, and the characters in the novels are different.
On the other hand, there is some relationship between *The First
Circle* and *Feast of the Conquerors* in that both have a character by the name of Nerzhin—Solzhenitsyn's *alter ego.* A
friend of Solzhenitsyn's has denied the existence of *Archipelag
Gulag* as a novel on its own. He explains that it is a collective
title Solzhenitsyn has given all his works dealing with the camp
theme—*One Day in the Life of Ivan Denisovich, The Love-Girl
and the Innocent, Cancer Ward* and *The First Circle*—and
probably also, *Feast of the Conquerors,* which never was intended for publication. From the same source we learn that
Solzhenitsyn considered *The First Circle* to be his last work
to exploit the camp theme.

In the summer of 1969, the writer Anatoli Kuznetsov (who
had been given a travel visa to gather material for a book on
Lenin) asked for political asylum in London. As a result of
his defection, which shook the Soviet Writers' Unions, the cultural politics became embittered. Possibilities for the cultural
elite to travel abroad became drastically limited, to mention but
one of the restrictions imposed on them. A campaign for "the
ideological education of the writers" was initiated. Meetings
were held at different levels. At a conference of the Writers'
Union of Moscow, grave accusations were made against writers
like Lidya Chukovskaya (who had written a bitter, frank, open

letter to Mikhail Sholokhov after the 23rd Party Congress),
Lev Kopolev (Solzhenitsyn's friend and fellow prisoner) and
Bulat Okudzhava. The three of them had been active in the
movement protesting against the treatment meted out to
Solzhenitsyn, and were also suspected of being involved in the
smuggling of literature. The essential criticism at these meetings
was, however, aimed at Solzhenitsyn. One such meeting was
held by the small Writers' Organization in Solzhenitsyn's native
town, Riazan, on November 4. A notice on the local billboard
said that the purpose of the meeting was to listen to "information by secretary Taurin of the Writers' Union of RSFSR about
the decision of the Secretariat of the RSFSR Writers' Union
to adopt measures to intensify the work in the ideological education of the writers."

Present at the meeting were Frants Taurin, Aleksandr
Kozhevnikov, the ideological secretary of the Party in the
Riazan district, Povaryonkin, an editor from a publishing house,
six members of the Riazan Organization and three representatives of local organizations.

Taurin's briefing took, according to the protocol, only a few
minutes, after which the meeting turned into an hour-long
presentation of charges against Solzhenitsyn. The meeting was
presided over by the Riazan writer Sergei Baranov since the
local chairman, Ernst Safonov, "had suddenly become ill with
appendicitis". Judging from the insinuating remarks made by
some participants, it was in order to escape responsibility for
what was going to happen. The grotesque proceedings might
be guaranteed a place in literary history—a fact which
Solzhenitsyn, well aware of his position, did not fail to comment
on. His own transcript of the proceedings follows:

Vasily Matushkin (Riazan). I cannot refrain from discussing
Comrade Solzhenitsyn's attitude to literature and to our Writers'
Organization. I personally bear some responsibility for this; for,
I once recommended him for membership of the Writers'
Union. So when criticizing him here today, I am consequently
judging myself. When *Ivan Denisovich* first came out, it was
hard to understand all of it. There were many things that could

not be liked. After Simonov's and Tvardovsky's reviews however, this aspect could not be discussed. After all, we were hoping that Solzhenitsyn was going to be a model for our organization. These expectations have not been fulfilled. Just consider his attitude to our Writers' Union. In all these years he has never been present. It is true that he attended the election meetings—but without uttering a word. One of our most important duties, according to the statutes, is to assist young writers—but he has not given any such assistance, and he has not taken any part in the discussions on the works of "newly hatched" writers. He has not done any *work* whatsoever. One has the painful feeling that he has an arrogant attitude toward our Writers' Organization and to our small literary achievements. Frankly speaking, all his latest creative works (it is true that we don't know much about them, that we have not read them and that we were not invited to the discussions) are totally conflicting with what the rest of us are writing. To us, there is a Fatherland and we can think of nothing more valuable. But Solzhenitsyn's works are published abroad and then they are all tossed on our country. His works are exploited to soil the name of our nation, and when Aleksandr Isaevich is advised how to answer he pays no heed. Even when an article on the matter is published in *Literaturnaya Gazeta,* he does not react—he considers himself too clever for that.

Sergei Baranov. Your time is up—ten minutes.

(Matushkin requests a prolongation, and is supported by Solzhenitsyn.)

Matushkin. The Writers' Union is an entirely voluntary organization. There are people who get published without being members of the Writers' Union. The statutes of the Union clearly state that the Union brings together people of the same opinion—people who are building Communism together, devoting their whole creative activity to Communism and are following the road to Socialist realism. So, there is no place for Solzhenitsyn in the Writers' Organization. Let him work alone. Sad as it might be, Aleksandr Isaevich, I must say that our paths are going in opposite directions and we must part.

Nikolai Rodin (who the town of Kasimov brought to the meeting in a hurry despite illness). I have nothing to add to what Vasily Semenovich [Matushkin] has already said. If we study the statutes of the Writers' Union and compare them to

Aleksandr Isaevich's activity as a citizen, we will find great differences. He has not followed the rules, and has not shown any consideration for our Union. There have been occasions when we have not found anyone to send the manuscript of a new author to for an opinion, and Solzhenitsyn has not written anything. I have many complaints about him.

Baranov. This is a very important question, and the Board of the Writers' Union is correct in bringing it up in time. In the Writers' Union, we must know each other well and help each other. But what would happen, if we ran off in different directions? Who would then educate our youth? Who would lead the literary clubs of which we have so many in factories and in the institutions? Vasily Semenovich was right in commenting on the question of Aleksandr Isaevich. His works are not familiar to us. In the beginning his works causes a lot of agitation. I have personally always seen the dark colors come through in *Ivan Denisovich.* Or, just take *Matryona's House*—where has one ever seen such a lonely woman (living with cockroaches and a cat) who did not get help from anyone—where does one find such a Matryona? Nevertheless, I had hoped that Aleksandr Isaevich would write things that people would want to read. But where does he publish his writings, and what are they about? That we don't know. We must demand more of ourselves and of each other. Solzhenitsyn has broken off with our organization and it is evident that we must part company with him . . .

Solzhenitsyn. I want to ask a question.

(His request is rejected.)

Yevgeni Markin (Riazan). It is harder for me to talk—harder than for anybody else. To face the truth, the whole question concerns Aleksandr Isaevich's membership of our organization. When he was admitted, I was not yet a member of the Union. I am worried for the following reason: the unprecedented oscillation of the pendulum from one extreme position to another. I was working for *Literatura i Zhizn* at the time it voiced unheard-of praise of Solzhenitsyn. Since then, things have gone the opposite way—I have not heard such conflicting opinions about anybody else. Such extremity will later affect the consciences of those people who make the decisions. Let us recall how Yesenin was defamed only to be praised to the skies later on; and now there are people who want to drown him again.

Let us remember the sharp condemnations after 1946. It is harder for me, than for anybody else, to sort things out. If Solzhenitsyn is going to be expelled now, only to be admitted later, and then expelled once more and admitted again, then I don't want to be party to it. Where will those who escaped the discussion today find a new appendix?—(referring to Safonov). There are great problems in our organization: the members of the Union cannot find apartments. For two years the Riazan Writers' Union was run by the bandit, Ivan Abramov, who wasn't even a member of the Union; he stuck political labels on us. I studied at the Literature Department together with Anatoli Kuznetsov. My intuition never fails. We did not like him because he was a hypocrite. My opinion is that there are two ways of interpreting the statutes of the Union; they are like a stick with two ends. Naturally, one would like to ask Aleksandr Isaevich why he has not participated in the public activities. Why has he not stepped forward and spoken in our press about the confusion the foreign press has created around his name? And why has he not told us about it? Why has Aleksandr Isaevich not even tried to explain it to his fellow writers so as to throw some light on the question? I have not read his new works. My opinion on the question concerning Aleksandr Isaevich's membership of the Union is that he is not a member of *Riazan's* Writers' Organization. I fully agree with the majority.

Nikolai Levchenko (Riazan). The question has essentially been straightened out by those comrades who have already spoken. I would like to put myself into Aleksandr Isaevich's position and figure how I would have acted. If all my creative work was being used abroad, what would I have done? Well, I would have come to my comrades and asked for advice. But Solzhenitsyn isolated himself. I join the majority.

Povaryonkin (Editor). For many years Aleksandr Isaevich has been staying away from the Writers' Union. He did not come to the election meetings but sent telegrams—I also agree with the majority. Was that really supposed to be a basic attitude? Gorky used to say that the Writers' Union is a collective organ—a social organization. Aleksandr Isaevich obviously joined the organization for other reasons: to get a membership card. The ideas expressed in his works are not of such standard as to help us build the Communist society. He is defaming our bright future. His mind is all dark. To introduce a wingless character like Ivan Denisovich—that can only be done by an ideological opponent. He has placed himself outside the Writers' Organization.

Solzhenitsyn asks once more if he can put a question to the meeting. The chairman suggests that he makes his speech instead. After a short discussion his request is finally granted.

Solzhenitsyn. I ask those members of the Union who have accused me of refusing to give my opinion of manuscripts and declining to appear in front of young writers, to give at least one example of such a case.

(The challenge remains unanswered.)

Matushkin. It is the duty of a member of the Writers' Union to work actively without waiting for an invitation, according to the statutes.

Solzhenitsyn. I can only regret, that there will be no stenographic script of this meeting, and that not even detailed notes are taken down. In spite of this, our meeting might be of some interest not only tomorrow but even after a week. By the way, three female stenographers were busy at the Secretariat of the Writers' Union, but despite the statement by the Secretariat that my notes were tendentious, the Secretariat has not yet been able to show the stenographic transcript of that meeting.

First of all I want to relieve Comrade Matushkin's conscience. I want to remind you, Vasily Semenovich [Matushkin], that you have never given me any recommendation whatsoever; in your capacity of secretary at that time you presented me only with blank questionnaires. During that period of excessive panegyric the RSFSR Secretariat was in such a hurry to admit me, that there was no time to gather recommendations or to let the primary Organization of Riazan first make me a member. Instead, they admitted me as a member themselves and even sent me a congratulatory telegram.

The charges made against me here, can be divided into two separate groups. The first one concerns the Riazan Organization, and the second, my whole literary future. About the first group of accusations I must tell you that not a single one of them has been accurate. Our secretary, Comrade Safonov, is not present here today. I have always informed him of every official action I have taken and of every letter I have written to the Congress or the Secretariat *the very day* it was done,

and I have asked him to keep all members of the Riazan Organization as well as our young writers informed. Did he not
show my letters to you? Was it because he himself did not want
to? Or was it because he had been forbidden to do so by Comrade Kozhevnikov here? I have not avoided any artistic contacts
with Riazan's Writers' Organization. On the contrary, I told
Safonov (and even insisted) to have my *Cancer Ward,* which
was discussed by Moscow's Writers' Organization, discussed in
Riazan too. I have copies of a letter on this matter. However,
for some reason, *Cancer Ward* has been kept secret to the members of Riazan's Organizations. I have also, in the same way,
always expressed my willingness to appear in person or speak
publicly, but I have never been allowed to do that because of
the fear that something would happen. And, with regard to my
"arrogant" attitude, I think it is ridiculous; none of you can
possibly remember any case, any phrase or behavior that might
be called arrogant. It has seemed to me, on the contrary, that
I have had very personal and friendly relations with all of you.
It is certainly true, that I have not been attending all meetings
at the Riazan Organization, but that is because I am not in
Riazan most of the time, but in the vicinity of Moscow, on the
outskirts of the city. Shortly after the publication of *Ivan
Denisovich* people urged me to move to Moscow, but I was
afraid I would not be able to concentrate on my work there,
and said no. However, when several years later I wanted to
move there, I was refused permission. I turned to the Moscow
Organization requesting to be registered there but the secretary,
V. I. Ilyin, replied that it was not possible and that I had to
remain in the Organization of the place mentioned in my passport as my native town. He said that it did not matter where
I was actually residing. That is why it has sometimes been difficult for me to come to the election meetings.

To discuss the charges generally, I still do not understand
what kind of a "reply" I was expected to give—a reply to *what?*
To the notorious article in *Literaturnaya Gazeta* where I was
set in opposition to Anatoli Kuznetsov (who asked for political
asylum in London shortly after the article was published) and
which said that his answer (and not mine) was the kind that
should be given to the West? I have nothing to "reply" to that
anonymous article.

The justification for my rehabilitation is questioned—by that
slyly elusive phrase "served his term"—you see, "served his

prison term and everything". There are lies about my novels, claiming that *The First Circle* contains "vicious slander against our social system"—but who has proved, demonstrated and illustrated that? Nobody knows the novels, but anything can be said about them. There are some minor distortions in the article; in addition to that the whole substance of my letter to the Congress has been twisted. And finally, this trite story about *Feast of the Conquerors*. By the way, it would be appropriate to wonder *from where Literaturnaya Gazeta* received the information about this play, how it got hold of it for reading, if *the only copy* is lying on the desk of the Security Service.

What, generally speaking, happens to my works is that if I repudiate any of them and don't want it to exist anymore—which was the case with *Feast of the Conquerors*—then great efforts are made to discuss and "analyze" it as much as possible. If I insist on having my works published—as has been the case with *Cancer Ward* and *The First Circle*—then they are hidden away and are not discussed.

Do I have to "reply" to the Secretariat? I have already answered all the questions put to me by the Secretariat, while the Secretariat has not answered a single one of my questions. I have not received any reply whatsoever to my letter to the Congress—neither with regard to its general nor its personal parts. It was considered insignificant compared to other problems at the Congress and was swept under the rug. I'm beginning to believe that the matter was deliberately delayed until the letter had been circulated widely for some weeks—and when it was published in the West, that was taken as a convenient excuse for not publishing it here.

Exactly the same method was used against *Cancer Ward*. As early as September, 1967, I energetically warned the Secretariat of the risk that the novel might appear abroad since it was already widely circulating in this country. So I hurriedly authorized the publication here, in *Novy Mir*. The Secretariat was still waiting. In the spring of 1968 there were certain indications of an imminent publication of the novel in the West. I turned to *Literaturnaya Gazeta, Le Monde* and *Unità* telling them in letters that I was prohibiting the publication of *Cancer Ward* and refused the Western publishing houses any right to publish it. And what happened? My registered letter to *Le Monde* did not reach its destination. The letter to *Unità*, which was sent through the famous Communist and publicist, Vittorio Strada, was taken away from him by the Customs—and I had to use my most subtle means to convince the Customs officials that it was in the urgent interest of our literature that this letter was published in *Unità*. However, in spite of all this, it was published in *Unità* a few days after this conservation, in the beginning of June; but *Literaturnaya Gazeta* was still waiting. *What* were they waiting for? For *nine* weeks, from April 19 until June 26, they kept my letter a secret. They waited for *Cancer Ward* to be published in the West. And when the novel appeared in the disgusting Mondadori edition, then, and *then* only, *Literaturnaya Gazeta* printed my protest together with its own rambling, anonymous article in which I was accused of not having protested *energetically enough or strongly enough* against the publication of *Cancer Ward*. So, why was *Literaturnaya Gazeta* dragging its feet for nine whole weeks? The purpose is obvious: let *Cancer Ward* appear in the West so it will be possible to condemn it and not pass it on to the Soviet reader. However, if my protest had been published in time, it might have stopped the publication of *Cancer Ward* in the West—two American publishers, Dutton and Praeger, for instance, abandoned their plans to publish the book as soon as they, in May 1968, heard *rumors* that I had protested against the publication of *Cancer Ward*. What would have happened if *Literaturnaya Gazeta* had published my protest without delay?

Baranov. Your time is up—ten minutes.

Solzhenitsyn. How can you speak about rules here? It is a vital question.

Baranov. But you can't have more—the rules . . . (Solzhenitsyn protests.) How much more time do you need?

Solzhenitsyn. I have a lot to say. Give me at least ten more minutes.

Matushkin. Give him three minutes.

(After a short consultation Solzhenitsyn is given ten more minutes.)

Solzhenitsyn. I have turned to the Ministry of Communications asking them to stop the *robbery* of my correspondence—letters, telegrams, printed matter—particularly from abroad—have not reached their destination or have been delayed—for example, when I wrote to my well-wishers who had sent me congratulations on my 50th birthday. But how do you like the idea that this *post robbery* is supported by none other than the Secretrariat of the Union of Soviet Writers? The Secretariat has not sent me one single letter or telegram out of the heap of mail addressed to me which it received on my birthday. They are still keeping all the mail without saying a word.

My entire correspondence is being censored—that's not enough—this illegal censorship is used with cynical frankness. So it was, for example, that the head of the Russian department of the Academy of Sciences was called by the secretary of the Frunze district, who informed him that my voice could not be recorded on tape at the Institute—he had received information, through a report sent to him by the censorship, that this had been done.

Now, to the accusation about having "distorted real life". Tell me: when and where, and in which theory of knowledge has the *expression* of the matter been considered more important than the matter itself? Possibly in the everyday philosophies but not in the materialistic dialectics. It will look as if what we are doing is not what is important but what people are saying about it; and it seems important that they don't say anything negative. We shall keep silent about what's going on then. But this is no solution. There is no reason to feel ashamed of villainy when you are merely talking about it; but there is every reason to when it is *being committed*. The poet Nekrasov has said:

One who lives in sorrow and anger
does not love his country

It is equally true that one who is always smoothly cheerful is indifferent to his country.

There has been talk about the pendulum. The oscillation of the pendulum is certainly significant, not only to me but to our entire lives: one wants to forget and conceal the Stalinist atrocities, not remind everybody about them. Is there any reason for reminding people about the past? This question was put to Leo Tolstoy by his biographer Biryukov. And Tolstoy (I am quoting Biryukov's *The Life of Tolstoy*) answered:

'If I had a serious illness and was cured and freed from it, it would always be a pleasure for me to talk about it. I would plainly not mention it, if I went on suffering and getting worse and I wanted to betray myself. We are ill—all of us. The form of the illness has changed but it is still the same illness; we only call it something else. . . . The illness we are suffering from is the killing of man. . . . If we would only recall the past and look straight into the eyes of the past—then the violence we are now committing would be disclosed.'

No, you will not succeed in keeping Stalin's crimes secret infinitely, and you will not succeed in working against truth infinitely. The question is one of crimes against millions of people—and they call for exposure. It might be a good idea to think about the moral effect on the young generation the concealing of these crimes will have. It will mean the corruption of millions of new people. The growing youngsters are not stupid. They understand perfectly well that there have been crimes committed by the millions and that they are passed over in silence; it's all 'hush-hush'. What is there then to stop us all from taking part in unjust acts? We'll have 'hush-hush' there too.

It remains to be said, that I don't retract one single word, one single letter, in my letter to the Writers' Congress. I'll end with the same words as the letter:

'I feel confident thinking that I will be able, under any circumstances, to fulfil my duty as an author, even more successfully and more undisputably from my grave than as a living person. Nobody will succeed in blocking the course of truth, and to promote that cause I am prepared even to accept death'.

I am ready to accept death much less expulsion from the Union.

But will these many lessons eventually teach us not to stop the writer's pencil in his lifetime? That policy has never, to this day, been a credit to our history.

Well, start voting—you are the majority. However, remember, that history of literature will take an interest in our meeting here today.

Matushkin. I have a question for Solzhenitsyn. How would you explain the fact that they are so interested in publishing you in the West?

Solzhenitsyn. And how do you explain the fact that they are so persistent in not wanting to publish me in my own country?

Matushkin. No, you have to answer me. The question was put to you. . . .

Solzhenitsyn. I have answered already. I have answered that I have more questions and I have presented them before—let the Secretariat answer mine.

Kozhevnikov (stops Matushkin from answering). Take it easy. Comrades, I don't want to interfere with your meeting and your decision. You are entirely independent. I want to protest, however, against the political implications which Solzhenitsyn is trying to force on us. We bring up one question, he another. All publications are at his disposal for answering the West, but he does not make use of this possibility. He does not want to give a retort to our enemies; he does not want to answer our enemies in his own words, without references to Nekrasov and Tolstoy. The Congress rejected your letter as unnecessary and ideologically incorrect. In your letter you were denying the leading role of the Party while we insist on it—on the leading role of the Party. I think that your former comrades in the Union have said the right thing—that we are not prepared to accept that! We must all march on time, in close formation, all together— not following the beats of a whip but our own conscience!

Taurin. It is now up to the RSFSR Secretariat to handle the matter. You are right. The most important thing is not to give reports about manuscripts or to lead literary groups. The most important thing is that you, Solzhenitsyn, have not objected to the exploitation of your name by the West. It can partly be explained by the *injustice* of your previous sentence and the hardships you have suffered. Occasionally, however, the future of the country must be put higher than your own. Every man is the architect of his own fortune. You must realize that nobody wants you down on your knees. The purpose of this meeting is to attempt to help you to refute the wrong statements made about you in the West. There, Solzhenitsyn is described as an extremely talented man playing the role of the enemy of his own country. People may in this struggle overshoot the mark, but I have been informed of what happened at the meeting of the Secretariat. The secretaries, and particularly, comrade Fedin asked you for some concessions and that you publicly denounce the excitement which has been stirred up in the West. This means a double damage: our country is slandered and a talented writer is taken away from us. The decision which will be made today will also be discussed by the RSFSR Secretariat.

Levchenko (reading from the typewritten resolution proposal). '. . . 2. The meeting considers Solzhenitsyn's behavior to be of an anti-social character fundamentally defying the purposes and duties of the Union of Soviet Writers.

Because of anti-social behavior, contrary to the purposes and duties of the Union of Soviet Writers, and grave violation of the fundamental rules of the charter of the Union of Soviet Writers, the *publicist* Solzhenitsyn is expelled from the Union of Soviet Writers.

We are asking the Secretariat to ratify the decision.'

Markin. I would like to hear the opinion of our secretary, comrade Safonov. Is he kept informed or not?

Baranov. He is ill. The meeting is competent to take a decision.

Five people voted for and one against the expulsion of Solzhenitsyn in the vote that ensued.

This development became generally known in Moscow in the days that followed and was even reported in carefully-worded terms by Western journalists. They were, however, not able to get the information confirmed by the Writers' Union; instead it was denied by an official—probably, so as not to mar the November 7 celebrations of the Revolution. After the holiday, *Literaturnaya Gazeta* carried a notice on November 12 informing the public of the meeting in Riazin in the following terms:

"The meeting unanimously pointed out that A. Solzhenitsyn's behavior is anti-social and is fundamentally defying the principles and duties, stipulated in the charter of the Union of Soviet Writers.

It is known that A. Solzhenitsyn's name and his works in the last few years have been actively used by the hostile bourgeois propaganda in a slander campaign directed against our country. A. Solzhenitsyn has not only failed to denounce this campaign publicly but has also—despite criticism from the Soviet public and repeated recommendations by the Union of Soviet Writers—contributed in fact, by certain actions and statements, to the anti-Soviet propaganda built up around his name.

On these grounds, the meeting of the Riazan Writers' Organization decided on the expulsion of A. Solzhenitsyn from the Union of Soviet Writers.

The Board of the RSFSR Writers' Union has approved the decision of Riazan's Writers Organization."

The same day Solzhenitsyn wrote this bitter and open letter to the Secretariat of the Russian Writers' Union:

"Shamefully trampling upon your own statutes in the mud, you have expelled me in my absence, with extreme haste and without even summoning me telegraphically, without even giving me the four hours I needed to get to Riazan to be present at the meeting. You have demonstrated openly that the decision preceded the 'discussion'. Were you afraid that you might have had to give me ten minutes to reply? I have been forced to make up for them with this letter.

Wipe the dust off the faces of the clocks—your clocks are slow! Draw the expensive, heavy drapes! You couldn't even imagine that it is getting light outside. These are not the same dumb, gloomy, hopeless times as when you, with the same servility, expelled Akhmatova. And it is not even the watchful, chilly times when you noisily expelled Pasternak. Was that shame not enough? Would you like to make it even worse? However, we are getting close to the hour when each one of you will try to erase your signatures under today's resolution.

You blind who are leading the blind! You do not even notice that you are walking in the opposite direction to what you have proclaimed. In this critical hour of our seriously ill society, you are incapable of proposing anything constructive, anything useful. All you have is your hatred, your watchfulness; I shall say only this: 'hold on and do not lose the grip!'

Your bombastic articles are falling apart, your vapidity is moving clumsily—there are no arguments, only voting and administrating. That is why neither Sholokhov nor the rest of you together dare answer the famous letter by Lidya Chukovskaya, the pride of Russian publicists. But the administrative screws are ready for her: how could she have the audacity to permit her unpublished book to be read? Once *powers that be* have decided not to publish you—then just surrender, suffocate and cease to exist! Do not give it to anybody to read!

They are also watching for an opportunity to expel Lev Kopelev, the veteran soldier, who has already been innocently imprisoned for ten years—but this time he is guilty of interfering on behalf of the persecuted, or disclosing a sacrosanct secret conversation with an influential person—of a breach of *official secrecy.* But how is it that you carry on such conversations that must be kept secret to the people? Are we not the ones who fifty years ago were promised that there would be no more secret diplomacy, secret talks, inconceivable secret appointments and replacements and that the masses would be informed of everything and be able to discuss it *openly?*

'The enemy listens'—is your excuse—these eternal and permanent 'enemies'—the convenient basis for your functions and your existence. As if there were no enemies when the promise about frankness was given. What would you do without 'enemies'? You could not exist without 'enemies'; hatred has become your barren atmosphere—a hatred that is not inferior to racism. However, in this way, the feeling for a homogeneous humanity is being lost—and its ruin is accelerated. Well, if the mass of Antarctic ice were to melt tomorrow and we were all turned into drowning humanity, into whose face would you then throw the 'class struggle'? There is no need to talk of the day when the remaining two-footed creatures would wander around, dying on the radioactive Earth.

All the same, it is time we remember that we first of all belong to humanity. *Thought and speech* make the world of humans different from the animal kingdom. And by physical necessity they must be free. Chain them, and we will return to animal life.

Frankness—honest and complete *frankness*—is the prime condition for the health of every society—for ours too. And he who does not wish our country to have frankness, is indifferent to his homeland and sees only to his own selfish needs. He who does not wish his country frankness, does not want to cure the illness but wants to repress it inwardly to have it rot there."

Following the expulsion, the campaign against Solzhenitsyn became unrestrained to the degree that there were even rumors, for some time, that the Authorities were planning to exile him from the country or even to bring up charges against him. The British magazine, *Private Eye,* went as far as to point out Pavel Licko as the main witness for the Prosecution.

Very few Soviet writers protested openly against the expulsion of Solzhenitsyn. Following the invasion of Czechoslovakia, the trial of many rebellious intellectuals, and the expulsions and dismissals of officials from the Party and the institutions, protests of this kind had become very hazardous.

The reaction abroad, however, was violent. Influential people belonging to the cultural elite protested in letters and telegrams. Of particular importance was the attitude of the leftist intellectuals.

The officials of the Writers' Union were still, as expected, constantly unavailable for protests.

On November 26 *Literaturnaya Gazeta* published a strong communiqué issued by the Secretariat of the Russian Writers' Union, and containing violent charges against Solzhenitsyn. He was accused, *inter alia,* of having "by deeds and statements joined in reality those, who are against the social order of the Soviet Union". He had allegedly also been promoted, by "enemies" in the West, to "leader of the political opposition in the Soviet Union".

The communiqué also carried a variation of the grotesque charge made by the former KGB head, Semichastny, who had claimed that Solzhenitsyn by not demanding any honorarium from Western pirate publishers was giving "material support" to capitalism. This time it said that the publication of Solzhenitsyn in the West was being used "to finance different subversive organizations". This was obviously a reference to the connections of the magazine *Grani* and the publisher Possev with the Russian exile organization NTS, which has been mentioned in several of the political trials ever since the Sinyavsky-Daniel affair.

Solzhenitsyn's letter of protest against his expulsion allegedly showed that he "had directly turned himself over to positions hostile to the cause of Socialism".

The communiqué ended in utterly malicious formulations which seemed to support the rumors that the Authorities were thinking of exiling the writer:

"Well, Solzhenitsyn has said what he wanted to say. The mask is torn off, the self-portrait is complete. By his 'open letters' he has demonstrated an attitude which is alien to our people and to our literature and has thereby confirmed that it was necessary, just and inevitable to expel him from the Union of Soviet Writers.

'Hold on and do not lose the grip!'—that is, according to Solzhenitsyn, the attitude of the Writers' Union to the writers.

But why now this 'hold on and do not lose the grip'? Nobody intends to do that, not even if Solzhenitsyn wants to go there, where his anti-Soviet works and letters are received with such enthusiasm each time."

In the weeks that followed the different Writers' Organizations throughout the country held new meetings, all condemning Solzhenitsyn and approving of his expulsion. These meetings also heard threats of various sanctions against writers who, on different occasions, had signed protest letters or who had works published abroad which had been prohibited by the Censorship Board in the Soviet Union.

On December 10 and 11, the Secretariats of the different Cultural Unions held a joint plenary session in Moscow. This meeting was attended by the most prominent cultural ideologists headed by the Party secretary Pyotr Demichev. In his address to the delegates he attacked various forms of revisionism in literature, particularly related to the shattered reformist Socialism in Czechoslovakia. Roger Garaudi and Solzhenitsyn were also attacked. The plenary session praised the local organizations of Moscow, and in particular Riazan, "which had demonstrated political maturity by the profound and principled condemnation of Aleksandr Solzhenitsyn's anti-social behavior. It is not by chance that the decision is supported by a unanimous literary opinion in the Soviet Republics, the districts and the territories".

Following this plenary meeting Solzhenitsyn practically turned into a "non-person"—unpublishable, unmentionable and, as anonymous as the politician who had personally intervened on his behalf in 1962.

Many signs, however, indicated that not all circles were satisfied with such a "liberal" solution. The police agents continued their burrowing. On New Year's Eve, 1969, the newly established Writers' Union in France published a communiqué in *Le Monde* revealing that an organization in Western Europe was offering the manuscript of a play by Solzhenitsyn to some publishers; it later turned out to be *Feast of the Conquerors*. The communiqué stressed that any publication of the play would immediately result in new charges against Solzhenitsyn and "might force him to leave his country".

That was evidently how Solzhenitsyn himself felt about his situation during the months following his expulsion from the Writers' Union. He was tormented by the Western pirate editions of his works, and he was seriously worried that tendentious material from his confiscated archives, in particular, *They Read Ivan Denisovich* (a resumé of the reactions of various groups of readers to the story, including the views of former camp inmates, camp guards, security policemen and present interns), *Answer to Three Students* and the play, *Feast of the Conquerors,* was being published and commented on in the West. Since this very compromising part of the smuggling had so obviously been organized by Soviet secret agents, he was forced to act drastically.

Contact was established between Solzhenitsyn and the Swiss lawyer, Fritz Heeb, in January 1970, and he became Solzhenitsyn's legal representative in the West. In March, Heeb wrote several West-European and American publishers who had published Solzhenitsyn. In a Zürich dated letter of March 5, Heeb states that he is authorized to declare the following:

1. My client has repeatedly tried to get his works published in his country. . . . With this purpose he has, without success, on repeated occasions turned to the Union of Soviet Writers for assistance.

2. Solzhenitsyn has publicly protested against the unauthorized publication of his works abroad. Since neither the Union of Soviet Writers nor Mezhdunarodnaya Kniga (a Soviet literary agency) has taken any action to protect his rights as an author, and since he now, as a result of his expulsion from the Writers' Union, has lost all possibilities of receiving such assistance, he has entrusted the protection of his rights outside the Soviet Union to his Swiss lawyer.

3. Solzhenitsyn has authorized his lawyer to: (a) declare as illegal every future publication without authorization, and to take action against misuse of his name, if so required by court action and legal proceedings against the originators of compromising statements; (b) with the help of competent experts study the quality of translations of Aleksandr Solzhenitsyn's works, new editions as well as reprints of already published works, and carry out necessary improvements; (c) prohibit adaptations for movie, radio and television.

4. Considering the vicious and false reports that have been spread, according to which my client's royalties have been handed over to subversive anti-Soviet organizations, I am authorized to state that royalties due Solzhenitsyn are untouched. After his death they will be disposed of according to his wishes.

5. All publishers are hereby informed that all publication of my client's works in the future can only be made after an authorization stipulated by contract with the writer or his legal representative.

Heeb's mandate has, as far as is known, been sincerely questioned only by the West German and British publishers who brought out the pirate editions of *August, 1914* in the fall of 1971. The Swiss lawyer rapidly gained respect in international publishing circles which saw him as an attorney who has acted energetically and correctly when it has been possible even though the mandate is not entirely realistic in all its aspects. For example, he was able to stop, in December 1970, the Swedish Broadcasting Corporation from broadcasting the play, *The Light That Is in You,* which was first published in the West by a Romanian exiled publisher. The Western publishers who owed Solzhenitsyn royalties do not seem to have hesitated to send them to the Swiss lawyer, often without being reminded.

For the moment, a little more than a year after Heeb's appearance on the scene, it seems as if he has been successful in his most urgent task: to prevent the publication of material which has been brought out from the Soviet Union for provocative purposes. Thus it was for instance that the publication of the play, *Feast of the Conquerors* stopped.

The Isolation

The consequence of Solzhenitsyn becoming a "non-person" following his expulsion from the Writers' Union was that he lived in isolation.

However, out of the almost total isolation in which he lived and worked for most of 1970, a sign of life—an extremely angry one—flashed on June 15. That was immediately after his friend, the famous gerontologist Zhorez Medvedev had been arrested and confined to a mental institution. Solzhenitsyn's protest was in the form of an open letter which spread rapidly among the intellectuals in the Soviet Union. He wrote:

"Without a warrant and without any medical reasons whatsoever, four militiamen and two physicians arrive in the home of a healthy man. The doctors state that he is mad, a militia major shouts: 'We are an *Instrument of Power!* Get up!' They twist his arms and take him to the mad house. This can happen to anyone of us tomorrow. It just happened to Zhorez Medvedev, geneticist and publicist, a man of subtle, precise and brilliant mind with a warm heart. (I am personally acquainted with his unselfish way of helping unknown, sick and dying people.) It is exactly for these many prolific talents that he is accused of abnormality: 'a split personality'! It is his sensitivity to injustice and stupidity that is being described as an aberration: 'poor adjustment to the social environment'! As soon as one thinks of anything else but what is *dictated,* it is taken as a sign of abnormality! Well-adjusted men all think the same. And it is unavoidable: even appeals from our most prominent scientists and writers bounce, like peas thrown against a wall.

Was it the first and only case? However, oppressing people without searching for real guilt (since the true motive is too

161

shameful to disclose) is becoming fashionable. Some victims are well-known, many more are unknown. Servile psychiatrists are violating their professional oaths and diagnosing as 'mental illness' care for social matters, extreme enthusiasm as well as exaggerated indifference, extremely brilliant talents as well as a total lack of gifts.

Plain common sense should be a restraining factor. Not a hair was touched on Chaadaev's head, although we have damned his persecutors for more than a century. It is time for us to clearly realize that freedom of thought, and locking up people in good health in mad houses equal *murder of the spirit,* a variation of the *gas chamber,* although even more cruel: the agony of the people who are being killed, is more horrible and more prolonged. Like the gas chambers, these crimes will *never* be forgotten, and everybody who has been involved in them, will be condemned for ever, in life as well as after death. Amidst this lawlessness, in which these crimes are committed, it is important to remember the limit beyond which man turns into a cannibal! It is short-sighted to believe that it is possible to live relying on violence alone and constantly ignoring the demurs of the conscience."

Solzhenitsyn's letter, probably to a high degree, influenced the release of Medvedev. He was discharged from the mental hospital shortly afterwards after a psychiatric commission set up by the Academy of Sciences had declared him in perfect health. The confinement of Medvedev had caused great anxiety among the Academy members.

When writing the protest letter against the Medvedev case Aleksandr Solzhenitsyn was staying in a "dacha" belonging to the famous cellist Mstislav Rostropovich, just outside Moscow. After his expulsion from the Writers' Union, it was totally impossible for him to stay in Riazan. The situation was further aggravated by complications in his family life; he was no longer living with his wife. He finished his new novel *August, 1914* in an annex to Rostropovich's villa. He started collecting the material for this novel when he was a high-school student in Rostov-na-Donu, before World War II, and the East Prussian landscape in the novel became familiar to him during the time preceding his arrest in February, 1945.

The novel was completed toward the end of October 1970, which coincided with the beginning of the fuss around the Nobel Prize.

The Nobel Prize

On October 8, 1970—a Thursday—the journalists crowded outside a particular door in the Nobel Library of the Swedish Academy earlier than usual. The famous clock struck one, but Karl-Ragnar Gierow, the Permanent Secretary, who always used to fling the doors open on the stroke of the hour, was almost a minute late. Then, all of a sudden he was standing there, wearing dark glasses and reading aloud in the spotlight:

"The Swedish Academy has today decided to award the Russian writer Aleksandr Solzhenitsyn this year's Nobel Prize for Literature".

The citation of the Academy read:

"For the ethical force with which he has pursued the indispensable traditions of Russian literature".

The journalists rushed off to the telephones. The news agencies flashed out the news over the wires. The telephone calls stirred up a particularly hectic activity at the Stockholm Tabloid Expressen, which for weeks had been running a campaign with the slogan: "The Nobel Prize to Solzhenitsyn!" A few hours before the announcement the staff had hesitated after hearing rumors of another possible candidate; now the portrait and biography of that candidate had to be thrown out of the frame to make place for Solzhenitsyn's.

A minute after 1 p.m., a telex message reached the Scandinavian journalists in Moscow. They were well prepared and knew that Solzhenitsyn was staying in the "dacha" belonging to the famous cellist Mstislav Rostropovich at Shukovka, 17 miles west of Moscow. Nevertheless, Solzhenitsyn was unreachable and was to remain so. The telegram from the Swedish

Academy did not reach him; it was sent to Riazan, where the author had not been living for a long time. The Norwegian journalist Per-Egil Hegge contacted one of Solzhenitsyn's closest friends who forwarded the message. However, Solzhenitsyn did not believe him; the Nobel Prize was to be announced on the third Thursday of October, not on the second—a false alarm again, just like the previous year!

Finally Hegge managed to get Rostropovich's secret telephone number. He called up at 1:45 p.m. The following conversation took place:

Hegge. Aleksandr Isaevich, I want to congratulate you on the Nobel Prize.
Solzhenitsyn. Where did you receive those reports?
Hegge. It has been officially announced by the Swedish Academy in Stockholm.
(Silence.)
Hegge. Would you like to comment on it?
Solzhenitsyn. No, I am not prepared to give any interviews.
Hegge. But the world is interested in your reaction, Aleksandr Isaevich.
Solzhenitsyn. Well, then I want to get some paper and a pencil and dictate a statement. It must be reported word for word. I don't want my words to be formulated differently.
(Silence. Solzhenitsyn is writing. Then he dictates:)
    "I am grateful for the decision. I accept the prize. If the decision is in my hands I intend to go and receive it personally on the traditional day. I am in good health. A trip would not hurt my health."
    (Hegge repeats the message and Solzhenitsyn confirms that it has been correctly understood.)
Hegge. Where are you staying now?
Solzhenitsyn. I don't want to tell you that. You may consider me unavailable. I don't intend to receive any foreign correspondents.
Hegge. Will you celebrate the event?
Solzhenitsyn. I think so. I had not expected a decision until a few days later. Where did you get my telephone number?
Hegge. From friends who told me that you did not believe the report.

The same night some of Solzhenitsyn's closest friends gathered at Rostropovich's. They toasted. Right after the first toast, however, Solzhenitsyn left the group and went over to the small wooden annex where he was staying. He went on writing as if nothing had happened but only that his strict working schedule had been upset.

As was the case with Pasternak the first Soviet reaction did not appear until 24 hours later. This time the reason probably was, that the leading officials of the Writers' Union were attending a conference in Arkhangelsk. On October 9, the Secretariat of the Union delivered the following message through Tass and a correspondent of *Izvestia:*

"As the public already knows, the works of this publicist which were taken abroad illegally and published there, have since long been used by reactionary circles in the West for anti-Soviet purposes.

The writers of the Soviet Union have on several occasions in the press stated their attitude to A. Solzhenitsyn's artistic work and behavior, which as announced by the Secretariat of the Board of the Writers' Union of RSFSR, conflict with the principles and duties of the voluntary Association of Soviet Literary Writers. The Soviet writers have expelled A. Solzhenitsyn from their Union. We know, that this decision is actively supported by the entire Soviet public.

It is regrettable that the Nobel Prize Committee has allowed itself to be drawn into an unworthy game, which by no means has been set to promote the spiritual values and the traditions of literature but has been dictated by speculative political considerations".

This first reaction was milder than expected. The most interesting aspect of it is that it reveals a genuine astonishment; the Secretariat did not even take time to find out which institution was to "to blame". As was the case twelve years earlier (when Pasternak was awarded the prize) the criticism was addressed to the Nobel Committee which has nothing at all to do with the choice of laureates.

Commenting on the reaction of the Secretariat, *Literaturnaya*

Gazeta wrote on October 14, that the members of the "Nobel
Committee", by referring to Solzhenitsyn's "ethical force" had
had his "anti-Soviet attitude" in mind. The daily *Sovietskaya
Rossiya* the same day described the decision as a "provocation"
and the motive as "plainly political", saying:

"The decision was not at all dictated by concern for Russian
literature, and we Soviet writers consider it as still another international act of an anti-Soviet nature."

The Soviet news agency APN said in an article, which simultaneously appeared in some newspapers in the West, that
Solzhenitsyn's award "most of all looks like a spitefully mixed
sensation in bad taste." The phrase about Solzhenitsyn's "ethical force" was said to "conceal the powerlessness of the
Academy members *vis à vis* the hard pressure of the anti-
Soviet propaganda". It went on to say that Solzhenitsyn's writings are "literarily and politically weak". He is pictured as a
"mainly average writer" who has put on dark glasses and
thereby deprived himself of the possibility of noticing the whole
color spectrum of the life of his country. The article continued:

"Because of his abnormal self-esteem, he has swallowed the
flattery by people who do not shun any means to fight the
Soviet system. As payment for his services, Solzhenitsyn has
seen his works compared in a ridiculous way to the writings
of the great Russian writers, although he must know that he,
when it comes to literary talent, is inferior to many living Soviet
authors. . . . In this way Solzhenitsyn has managed to make
business, and not tragedy, of his solitude."

Again taking the Swedish Academy to task the article
continued:

"The members of the Swedish Academy have discredited the
Nobel Prize. Our moral standards might however, be too high
for some Academy members. The Nobel laureates include
André Gide, who was condemned by his own, and other people,
for collaborating with the Hitlerites."

This flow of indignation in the Soviet press, however, slowed
down gradually and came to a complete stop a week after the
Nobel Day on December 10.

It turned out that *not one* important writer could be persuaded to sign a protest against the Nobel Prize; the literary profession had been too burnt by the Pasternak scandal. Nevertheless there were reports that the small group of activists, who had led the campaign against Solzhenitsyn since 1964, had made a desperate move to discredit the literary Nobel award. Members of this group called upon Mikhail Sholokhov, probably on their own initiative, urging him to reject the prize which he had received with such a warm official approval in his country. Sholokhov flatly refused.

After this the Soviet press reported almost exclusively negative reactions abroad, which as a matter of fact were extremely few. The Soviet press gave no hints whatsoever that Solzhenitsyn's Nobel Prize in reality had been applauded with unprecedented unanimity throughout that part of the world where *Cancer Ward* and *The First Circle* had been published. The Soviet press, however, showed more enthusiasm in publishing the indiscretions made by the Academy member Artur Lundkvist in an interview with the Stockholm evening newspaper *Aftonbladet* on December 10, the Nobel Day; these were published by the news agency Tass as a "declaration". The Tass report which was printed by *Pravda* the following day, read:

"The Swedish writer and Academy member Artur Lundkvist has declared that he considers the decision of the Academy to award A. Solzhenitsyn this year's prize as incorrect.

A. Lundkvist emphasized in an interview with the newspaper *Aftonbladet* that a decision like this will lead 'to conflicts that have nothing to do with literature. The enemies of the Soviet Union have been given a good excuse to instigate anti-Soviet feelings', he said.

'I have never disclosed how I voted when Solzhenitsyn was given the prize. However, I think it is a mistake that he received the award.'

Thus, Lundkvist summarized his opinion.

In reality it was well-known in Stockholm that Lundkvist had been strongly opposed to Solzhenitsyn's candidacy since 1969. According to very reliable information the Union of Soviet

Writers was awaiting the prize decision that year very anxiously. When the award finally went to Samuel Beckett the Soviet literary officials did not hesitate any longer. Only a few days after the announcement the Writers' Union of Riazan summoned its inquisitorial meeting at which Solzhenitsyn was expelled from the Union.

In 1970 the votes for Solzhenitsyn's candidacy evidently were seventeen to one. None of the seventeen had any doubts about Solzhenitsyn's literary qualifications, and besides, they had become convinced that the prize could not possibly further aggravate the writer's situation. It was this cautiousness and consideration that had stopped them from giving Solzhenitsyn the prize the year before.

There were many signs indicating that Solzhenitsyn, at the beginning was prepared to go to Stockholm in December. His friends advised him to apply for a passport to go abroad as soon as possible, but he did not even get started with the formalities. The stronger the new campaign against him grew, the more cautious he became, and he felt a grip of fear for being trapped. East European diplomats in Stockholm had hinted that the Authorities would be prepared to give Solzhenitsyn a passport if he asked for one, and similar assurances had been given to the writer's friends in Moscow; on the other hand there were no indications that they would allow him to return.

There were other reasons for his decision, toward the end of November, not to make the trip—the finishing touches to his novel *August, 1914,* and some personal problems: the divorce from his first wife and the advanced pregnancy of his future wife (Natalya, a young mathematician). For these reasons he did not consider it worth spending time visiting the offices of the passport authorities and the Party.

He wrote the following letter to the Swedish Academy and the Nobel Foundation on December 27:

I have already, in my telegram to the Academy secretary, expressed my gratitude, and want to do it once more, for the honor showed me by awarding me the Nobel Prize. Within me, I share it with those of my predecessors in Russian Literature, who due to the hard conditions of the past decades, did not live long enough to receive such an award or in their lifetime were not known through translations to the reading world or even to their countrymen—in the original.

In the same telegram I announced my intention to accept your invitation to come to Stockholm, even if I could foresee the humiliating procedure which was waiting for me and is established in our country for every trip abroad—the special forms to be filled out, the personal reports to be obtained from the Party Organizations (even for nonmembers) and the instructions about expected behavior.

The hostile attitude to my award which has been demonstrated by the press in my country in the past weeks, and the fact that my books, now as before, are being discriminated against (those who read them are dismissed from their jobs or expelled from their Institutes) make me believe that my trip to Stockholm will be used to separate me from my native country, or simply prevent me from returning home.

On the other hand, I understand from the material you have sent me concerning the arrangements connected with the handing over of the prize, that the Nobel ceremony includes much that is ceremonial and formal, which tires me and is strange to my way of life and character. The factual part however—the Nobel lecture—is not part of the ceremony. In later telegrams and letters you have expressed concern about the turmoil which could arise from my presence in Stockholm.

Considering this and taking into account your kind assurance that it is not an absolute condition to be personally present to receive the prize, I have preferred for the present moment, not to apply for permission to go to Stockholm.

If the form is acceptable to you, I could receive the Nobel diploma and the medal from your representatives in Moscow at a time suitable to you and myself. I am prepared, in accordance with the statutes of the Nobel Foundation, to give my Nobel lecture or send it to you within six months counting from October 10.

This is an open letter and I have no objections that you make it public.

Solzhenitsyn handed over the letter personally when he visited the Swedish Embassy in Moscow on November 27.

In his book *Solzhenitsyn Cannot Come* (Stockholm 1971) the Norwegian journalist Per-Egil Hegge has given a highly critical account of what happened at this and at a second visit (December 2). His book shed a rather merciless light on the actions of Ambassador Gunnar Jarring and the Embassy officials in this controversial affair. Obviously anxious not to harm Swedish-Soviet relations, the Swedish diplomats seemed willing, in their official capacities, to play only a minimal part when it came to handing over the prize insignia to Solzhenitsyn. This made it far too poor and Solzhenitsyn could not accept the ceremony as worthy.

Solzhenitsyn confirmed the essence of Hegge's criticism in a letter in the fall of 1971. The Nobel laureate asked rhetorically—after Premier Olof Palme and Foreign Minister Krister Wickman had engaged in a heated debate in Sweden—whether his Nobel Prize was some kind of "stolen goods" that could be handed over to him only secretly in Ambassador Jarring's office.

Toward the end of the year 1971, it became evident that the Swedish Embassy was not prepared to oblige the massive Swedish public opinion and arrange a more fitting ceremony in the Embassy or in the residence of the Ambassador. What had been possible a few years earlier, when the official poet laureate of the Soviet Union, Mikhail Sholokhov, received the award, now turned out to be completely impossible—for the prize was awarded to a man whose name was not even to be mentioned by the Soviet press.

A few days after the Nobel ceremony in Stockholm, Solzhenitsyn was attacked in a prominently displayed article in *Pravda* (December 17). The article said that the harbingers of anti-Communism "with the silent approval of Solzhenitsyn" had created the turmoil around his name. Attention was once more drawn to *Feast of the Conquerors,* together with *The First Circle* and *Cancer Ward* which were all lumped together under the label of "libelous pamphlets", which are "degrading the deeds and progress of our country and the dignity of Soviet men". Also, Solzhenitsyn was charged with attempt to blackmail the Writers' Union. He had allegedly "made threats that his anti-Soviet works would find their way abroad if they were not published".

The Nobel Committee was once more attacked for being misled by "the anti-Soviet speculators who have been praising Solzhenitsyn to the skies, not because of his so-called talent but because he has been defaming Soviet life".

After this article, however, the direct attacks on Aleksandr Solzhenitsyn ceased. His name was not mentioned in any of the speeches at the 24th Party Congress in the spring of 1971, although Mikhail Sholokhov promised "thorough cleanup" at the forthcoming Writers' Congress. The long report presented by Secretary General Leonid Brezhnev on March 30, also clearly showed that there was no relief to be expected by writers with Solzhenitsyn's type of critical attitude to the society:

"The Party and the People have not and will not ignore attempts—whatever direction they come from—to blunt our ideological arms and soil our banner. If a literary man slanders Soviet life and assists our ideological opponents in their struggle against Socialism, then he deserves one thing only—the disdain of the society."

Nevertheless, the Solzhenitsyn case was not discussed at the Writers' Congress in the summer of 1971. For unknown reasons Mikhail Sholokhov was not present at the Congress, and it is not known whom the "cleanup" was intended for.

Solzhenitsyn's name was not even mentioned during the Congress.

At about the same time that the Congress convened in Moscow the Russian emigrant publishing house (YMCA) in Paris came out with Aleksandr Solzhenitsyn's novel, *August, 1914,* the first part of the trilogy on World War I, which he had been gathering material for since his school years.

The "Appendix" to the novel clearly proves that Solzhenitsyn had authorized this edition. It is also known from other sources, that this publishing contract was handled through his Swiss lawyer Heeb.

The transaction was probably without precedence in Soviet

history. It is not known what made Solzhenitsyn—who earlier, had been so energetically trying to protect himself against the Western editions of *Cancer Ward* and *The First Circle* for instance—directly allow Western publishers to publish this novel, which in the spring of 1971 had been turned down by Soviet publishing institutions. By this action, Solzhenitsyn believed he could at least guarantee the Western copyright and a publication (in Russian and other languages) without the distortions and mistakes that befell so many of his works due to the haste and competition the publishers were in to get out translations in the leading languages.

In reality he was not safe even now. Not all Western publishing houses accepted the Bern convention about the rights of Soviet authors. A Russian pirate edition was published by the Romanian exiled publisher, Flegon, in London in the summer of 1971. The same publisher also announced his intentions of bringing out an English translation before the end of the year; the British publishing house that had obtained the rights to publish a translation (Bodley Head) had, like other copyright holders, agreed not to publish the book until August 1972 (this was to guarantee thorough interpretations of the novel). Shortly afterward a translation of the novel was published by Langen-Müller Verlag in West Germany (although the copyright there had been obtained by the publishing company Luchterhand).

Solzhenitsyn's unusual policy with *August, 1914* obviously marked an entirely new phase in his situation as a literary Nobel laureate, banned from the literary organizations of his own country. A world-famous publicist, he was "anonymous" in his own country: a moral monolith, he was literarily and economically exploited in the West.

Appendix

Following the Nobel Prize announcement Aleksandr Solzhenitsyn, over and over again, became the center of sometimes dramatic and often mysterious incidents. The Soviet press maintained a wall of silence around him until early January 1972. This did not mean, however, that they had decided to leave him alone. Occasionally, his voice could be heard through unofficial channels: a voice full of uncompromising indignation but also, with melancholy humor and irony.

In an open letter to the Security Minister Yuri Andropov and Premier Alexei Kosygin on August 13, 1971, he protested against a strange incident in his summer house of Rozhdestvo, outside Moscow. His friend Aleksandr Gorlov had visited the house, which was unoccupied, to get some spare-parts for Solzhenitsyn's car. There, he surprised a group of plain-clothes men, who evidently had broken into the house. They arrested him and ill-treated him, then demanded that he sign a document promising to keep silent about the incident. He refused. In the weeks that followed Gorlov was called up for interrogation many times. According to reports in the Russian underground press ("samizdat") Solzhenitsyn's letter of protest had the effect of making the district's Police Commissioner apologize to Gorlov.

Solzhenitsyn forcefully intervened against the cunning slander in the West against the Swiss lawyer Fritz Heeb, who had arranged among other things the copyright of *August, 1914.* Solzhenitsyn also supported Heeb and the copyright holders Luchterhand Verlag (West Germany) and Bodley Head (London) in their lawsuits against the pirate editions of the novel published by Langen-Müller and Flegon. The distribution of these pirate editions was halted by a court decision in the fall of 1971.

That fall the writer also continued his partly open correspondence with the Permanent Secretary of the Swedish Academy, Karl Ragnar Gierow, about arrangements for giving out the prize insignia. As a result of the unwillingness of the Swedish Ambassador to Moscow, Gunnar Jarring, to arrange a ceremony which was acceptable to Solzhenitsyn, Gierow offered to give out the insignia himself toward the end of the year in a private apartment in Moscow suggested by Solzhenitsyn. This was during the Russian Easter of 1972. Gierow's and Solzhenitsyn's intentions with this ceremony were to close the painful circle of anxious objections, detailed scholastic interpretations and diplomatic considerations (regarding Soviet-Swedish relations) which the Swedish Embassy had surrounded itself with in order not to get too involved in this controversial Nobel Prize affair.

The ceremony was scheduled for April 9. Gierow and Solzhenitsyn were both convinced that it would take place. However, on April 4, Gierow received the surprising news that the Soviet Authorities had rejected his application for a travel visa. Solzhenitsyn made it clear in a very indignant statement that he now considered the whole Nobel Prize matter closed. He declared that he was bequeathing the insignia to his son.

Other circles too, seemed to close during this peculiar month of December, in Aleksandr Solzhenitsyn's life.

Aleksandr Tvardovsky, his friend, his discoverer and supporter died on December 18. Solzhenitsyn made one of his rare public appearances at Tvardovsky's funeral at the Novodevichy Cemetery in Moscow. The former editor of *Novy Mir* was buried not far from the grave of the late Nikita Khrushchev who had died only a few months earlier—the politician, who at the height of his power, personally sanctioned Solzhenitsyn's debut. In picking a single flower from one of Tvardovsky's wreaths and putting it on Khrushchev's grave, Solzhenitsyn made a symbolic gesture marking the definite end of the literary "thaw".

Solzhenitsyn's unprecedented policy—to send out the manuscript of *August, 1914* quite openly—brought a new development to his situation as an author and as a private person. However, the reaction to this was slow in his own country, perhaps pending the outcome of the strange events that were taking place in London and West Germany around the new manuscript.

As soon as the Flegon pirate edition (a copy of the YMCA original) came out, rumors started circulating that a new "Solzhenitsyn affair" was developing in the Soviet Union. In mid-July, 1971 Michel Gordey wrote in *France-Soir*, that he had received information that Solzhenitsyn's situation had been further aggravated by Flegon's pirate edition. By connecting Solzhenitsyn with a publisher who, for a long time, had been specializing in publishing indisputably anti-Soviet literature, the Soviet Authorities could easily accuse the writer of hurting the Soviet Union. Reports of this kind were also published by many other newspapers abroad.

Within a few weeks Solzhenitsyn's Swiss lawyer, Heeb, had also been drawn into the picture. The "pirate publishing company" Langen-Müller challenged Heeb's right to represent Solzhenitsyn. A newspaper in Düsseldorf (*Express*) hinted that Heeb was guilty of large-scale "swindle". Meanwhile rumors were circulating in Paris that *August, 1914* after all, would be published in the Soviet Union—rumors which probably were spread to further undermine Heeb's mandate and prestige.

Solzhenitsyn categorically rejected these rumors in a letter, dated September 3. Solzhenitsyn declared in his letter addressed to Heeb that he was prepared to announce publicly and with emphasis that he highly appreciated Heeb's honesty and extraordinary business talents and that he could not possibly ask for a better lawyer. Solzhenitsyn also sent out a similar unequivocal declaration of his trust in Heeb through the Norwegian journalist Per-Egil Hegge.

But still in November, the Romanian exiled publisher Flegon was challenging Solzhenitsyn's right, before a court in London, to make business agreements *according to Soviet law* with foreign publishers, and maintain a legal representative abroad. Flegon's argument was rejected by the court, which stopped the distribution of the pirate editions. So also had a West German court decided in favour of Solzhenitsyn.

Obviously, this was a victory for Heeb and the copyright holders in West Germany and England. To Solzhenitsyn personally, it probably meant that planned attempts to associate him with an anti-Soviet publisher were put off. But the fact remained that two Western publishers before legal courts in the West had been using *Soviet* judicial interpretations and had publicly expressed charges against Solzhenitsyn based on *Soviet* law.

In some infamous way, it turned out that the novel *August, 1914,* too, was very useful as a weapon against the writer personally. With its help, the campaign against Solzhenitsyn's person was to be pushed to its utmost: far back to his birth and social origin.

This campaign was obviously part of a major campaign for ideological streamlining which was a result of the so-called November Plenum of the Central Committee in 1971.

Interwoven in the crowded gallery of people in *August, 1914* is what seems to be the family chronicle of Solzhenitsyn. Right in the first chapter we meet Isaaky Lashenitsyn who evidently has many characteristics of the writer's own father, Isai Semenovich Solzhenitsyn. Some other relatives are also pictured in the book; the names are only slightly changed, in some cases not at all.

In December of 1971, the West German magazine *Stern* published what allegedly was an interview with the 82 year-old Irina Shcherbak, living in Georgiyevsk and a sister-in-law of Solzhenitsyn's mother, Taisya.

In the "interview" (the authenticity of which has been questioned by Solzhenitsyn himself) she identifies herself with Irina Tomchak in the novel and even "unveils" the identities of many other people. She claims for instance, that Solzhenitsyn's mother was the daughter of "the estate-owner Zakhar Shcherbak" (Zakhar Tomchak in the novel). Solzhenitsyn's father, Isai, is

described as the son of "a rich land owner", Semeon Solzhenitsyn. Irina even hints that Isai who "officially" was declared
dead through a hunting accident a few months before Aleksandr
Solzhenitsyn's birth, "obviously" committed suicide in the
rolling chaos of the civil war. Irina herself brought a huge
fortune when she married Roman Shcherbak (the novel's
Roman Tomchak).

An abbreviated and tendentiously edited version of this "interview" was reproduced in *Literaturnaya Gazeta* on January
12, 1972 together with some commentaries, which all conclude
that *August, 1914* is an "anti-Soviet" book despite the fact that
the scene was set in pre-Soviet time.

Literaturnaya Gazeta also filled out the "interview" with
some observations from the village of Sablya, where Solzhenitsyn's grandfather Semeon Yefimovich Solzhenitsyn, and his
father Isai Semenovich had lived. According to the newspaper
reports his late grandfather owned, by the turn of the century,
over 5,000 acres of land and about 20,000 sheep. He also employed more than 500 people. The grandfather lived with his
four sons—Isai, Vasily, Konstantin and Ilya—and his daughter
Maria, on two farms. *Literaturnaya Gazeta* identifies one more
living relative of Solzhenitsyn's: Ksenya Zagorina, a daughter
of the writer's uncle Vasily and today a *kolkhoz* worker at
Sablya.

The very next day, January 13, Solzhenitsyn protested
angrily in a letter, against the tendentious reporting about his
origin and against the allegations that *August, 1914* was in fact
an attack against the Soviet Union, disguised in historical
form. At the same time he accused the Soviet feature bureau,
APN, for having more or less made up the interview with Irina
Shcherbak for the West German magazine. He also denied that
his parents and ancestors had been particularly rich people.

It is certainly questionable why *Literaturnaya Gazeta* circulated with such delight the reports carried by *Stern* to the Soviet
public who for years had not seen any biographical information
about Solzhenitsyn.

"They were a family of uncivilized people", the article about the Solzhenitsyn family began in *Literaturnaya Gazeta* (but not in *Stern*). Already in the first paragraph, the magazine took the opportunity to draw attention to speculations in the *Stern* article that Solzhenitsyn had "cunningly used an experienced technique to avoid punishment for anti-Soviet activity: he sets the action in pre-Revolutionary time. The reader understands immediately, however, that the writer, in describing historical events, is referring to current problems".

Commenting on the *Stern* article, *Literaturnaya Gazeta* explains that "we are naturally far from looking for a direct, vulgar sociological connection between, on the one hand, a person's origin, his milieu during adolescence and his education, and on the other hand, his activity as an adult". It is obvious, however, that it is exactly this parallel the magazine wants its readers to draw.

By this interview, the campaign to discredit Aleksandr Solzhenitsyn had in fact advanced one more step. He was now described as the offspring of capitalists and landowners, who were the "alien" and "socially hostile" elements overthrown by the Revolution. This version was spread in the Soviet Union in the first months of 1972.

So, it looked as if one more circle was closing: the slander campaign which started almost at the same time as the central press in Moscow, in the winter of 1962, declared that a new literary figure had made his entrance on the literary scene and that it had "become utterly clear that it would no longer be possible to write the way we were writing only a short time ago".

Bibliography

Solzhenitsyn: *One Day in the Life of Ivan Denisovich*, Moscow
    1962
    An Incident at the Krechetovka Station, Moscow 1963
    Matryona's House, Moscow 1963
    For the Good of the Cause, Moscow 1963
    Prose Poems, Frankfurt/Main 1964
    Linguistic Essay, Moscow 1965
    Zakhar Kalitá, Moscow 1966
    Cancer Ward, Milan, Frankfurt/Main, London, Paris
    1968
    The First Circle, Belgrade, New York, London 1968
    The Right Hand, Frankfurt/Main 1968
    The Light That Is in You, London 1968
    The Easter Procession, Frankfurt/Main 1968
    Answer to Three Students, Paris 1969
    They Read Ivan Denisovich, Frankfurt/Main 1969
    The Love-Girl and the Innocent, Frankfurt/Main 1969
    August, 1914, Paris 1971

Berger: *Art and Revolution*, London 1969

Blomqvist: *Soviet Literature After Stalin*, Stockholm 1968

Blomqvist-Ljunggren: *Soviet Protest*, Stockholm 1969

Conquest: *The Great Terror*, London 1968

Yevtushenko: *Autobiographie précoce*, Paris 1963

Guttenberger: *Bestraft mit Weltruhm* (*Punished By World
    Fame*), Frankfurt/Main 1970

Hayward-Crowley: *Soviet Literature in the Sixties*, London
    1965

Johnson: *Khruschchev and the Arts*, Cambridge, Mass. 1965

Kratkaya literaturnaya entsiklopediya 1–5, Moscow 1962–68

Labedz: *Solzhenitsyn,* London 1970

Mandelshtam, N.: *Vospominaniya,* New York 1970

Medvedev, Zh.: *The Medvedev Papers: The Plight of Soviet Science,* London, Basingstroke 1970

Mihajlov: *Leto moskovskoje 1964,* Frankfurt/Main 1966

Nielsen-Stokkeby: *Der Fall Solschenitsyn (The Solzhenitsyn Case),* Frankfurt/Main, Hamburg 1970

Peltnev: *A. I. Solzhenitsyn* (in Russian), Munich 1970

Schiller: *Zwischen Moskau und Jakutsk (Between Moscow and Yakutsk),* Hamburg 1970

Sjeklocha-Mean: *Unofficial Art in the Soviet Union,* Berkeley, Los Angeles 1967

Slonim: *Soviet-Russian Literature,* New York 1967

von Ssachno: *Der Aufstand der Person (The rebellion of the Individual),* Berlin 1965

von Ssachno-Grunert: *Literatur und Repression (Literature and Repression),* Munich 1970

Chetvertyi siezd pisatelei SSSR, stenogr. otchet, Moscow 1968

Tra autoritarismo e sfruttamento, Milan 1968

Articles, reviews, interviews, etc. from newspapers and magazines, essentially: *Novy Mir* (Moscow), *Literaturnaya Gazeta* (Moscow), *Okchabr* (Moscow), *Yunost* (Moscow), *Problemy mira i sotsializma* (Prague), *Kulturny Zivot* (Bratislava), *Grani* (Frankfurt/Main) *Problems of Communism, Osteuropa, Survey, Le Monde, New York Times, The Bookseller, The Times, L'Unità.*

Index

Abakumov, Victor (former head of the KGB executed in 1954), 33, 91, 108
Abashidze, Irakli (Secretary of the Writers' Union), 108
Abdumomunov, Toktobolot (Secretary of the Writers' Union), 98, 108
Abramov, Ivan, 146
Akhmadulina, Bella (poetess), 7, 86, 87
Akhmatova, Anna (poetess, died 1966), 3, 7, 89, 90, 107, 111, 155
Adzhubei, Alexei (former editor of *Izvestia*, son-in-law of the late N. Khrushchev), 2
Aksyonov, Vasily (author), 8, 58, 93
Alliluyeva, Svetlana (Stalin's daughter, living in the U.S.), 87, 107, 108, 125
Antokolsky, Pavel (poet), 7, 94
Antonov, Sergei (author), 94
Asanov, Nikolai (author), 84

Babel, Isaak (author), 16, 91
Bacon, Francis (English statesman and philosopher), 111
Baklanov, Grigori (author), 29, 49, 64, 85, 93
Balter, Boris (author), 93
Barabash, Yuri (critic), 61
Baranov, Sergei (author), 143, 144, 150
Baruzdin, Sergei (author), 97, 108–110
Beckett, Samuel (author, Nobel Prize laureate), 170
Bek, Aleksandr (author), 99
Belinkov, A. (author), 85
Belutin, Elya (painter), 5, 50
Berger, John (British art critic), 6
Beria, Lavrenti (former head of the State Security, executed 1953), 33, 91, 109
Beriozko, Georgi (author), 83, 86
Biryukov, Pavel (Lev Tolstoy's biographer), 151

Bondaryev, Yuri (author), 30
Borisoglebsky, V. V. (Chief Justice of the Military Collegium of the Supreme Court), 39
Borshchagovsky, Aleksandr (author), 84
Brezhnev, Leonid (Secr. general of the Communist Party), 80, 119, 126, 173
Brovka, Petrus (author), 108
Bukhanov, Viktor (journalist), 55
Budenny, Semeon (late Marshal), 15
Bulgakov, Mikhail (author), 7, 89, 90
Bunin, Ivan (author, Nobel laureate), 7, 89
Burkovsky, Boris (Captain), 63
Bykov, Vasil (author), 93

Chagall, Marc (painter), 3
Chaadaev, Pyotr (19th century philosopher), 162
Chakovsky, Aleksandr (editor of Literaturnaya Gazeta), 56
Chalmayev, V. (critic), 61
Chapchakhov, V. (critic), 54
Chukhrai, Grigori (movie director), 57
Chukovskaya, Lidya (authoress), 30, 142, 155
Chukovsky, Kornei (author), 53, 64

Daniel, Yuli (author, sentenced in 1966 to five years imprisonment with hard labor for smuggling manuscripts), 79, 138, 157
Dar, David (author), 94
Demichev, Pyotr (Party Secretary for ideological matters), 76, 94, 158
Diakov, Boris (author), 64
Dolotsev (Colonel of the Military Collegium), 39
Dostoevsky, Feodor, 89
Dremov, A. (critic), 62
Dubcek, Alexander (former Party leader, Czechoslovakia), 124

Dudintsev, Vladimir (author), 9, 87
Dymshits, Aleksandr (author), 49

Ehrenburg, Ilya (author), 4, 6, 12, 51, 53, 57, 64, 87
Eisenstein, Sergei (movie director), 53
Elsberg, Yakov (critic), 2

Falk, Robert (painter), 5, 51, 52
Fedin, Konstantin (first secretary of Writers' Union), 18, 43, 44, 96, 104, 111, 112, 131, 153
Fomenko, Lidya (critic), 54, 55
Freifeld, A. A. (lecturer), 102

Garaudi, Roger (French leftist), 158
Gide, André (author, Nobel laureate), 168
Gierow, Karl-Ragnar (Permanent Secretary of the Swedish Academy), 165, 176
Giordano, Bruno, 103
Gonchar, Oles (author), 66
Gorbatov, Aleksandr (Army General), 107
Gorky, Maxim, 3, 106, 146
Grakhovsky, Sergei (author), 108
Grin, Aleksandr (author), 91
Grossman, Vasily (author), 91
Gudzenko, Aleksandr (former camp prisoner), 62
Gumilev, Nikolai (poet), 89

Heeb, Fritz (Swiss lawyer), 74, 159, 175
Hegge, Per-Egil (Norwegian journalist), 166–172
Hitler, Adolf, 108
Hoxha, Enver (Albanian Party leader), 10
Husak, Gustav (Czechoslovakian Party leader), 68

Ilyin, V. I. (Secretary of RSFSR's Writers' Union), 148
Ilyichov, Leonid (former Party secretary), 53, 56
Iskander, Fazil (author), 93

Jarring, Gunnar (Swedish Ambassador to Moscow), 172

Kabo, Liubov (author), 85
Kaganovich, Lazar (politician during the Stalin era), 2
Kandinsky, Vasily (painter), 3

Karyakin, Yuri (critic), 19, 64, 68–70, 85
Karpov, S. S. (scientist), 31
Kashkadamov, N. (journalist), 52
Katayev, Valentin (author), 8, 93
Kaverin, Venyamin (author), 64, 93, 113, 117
Kazakov, Yuri (author), 6, 87
Kedrina, Zoya (authoress), 84
Kerbabaev, Berdi (Secretary of Writers' Union), 109
Khlebnikov, Velemir (poet), 7
Khrushchev, Nikita (former head of Party and government), 2–13, 29, 36, 44–45, 49–53, 56–59, 65–69, 79, 125
Kliuyev, Nikolai (poet, died in Siberia 1937), 89
Kochetov, Vsevolod (editor of Okchabr), 2, 62
Kogan, V. (physicist), 31
Konetsky, Viktor, 94
Konov (Colonel of the Military Collegium), 39
Konotop, Vasily (Party secretary, Moscow), 80
Kopelev, Lev (author), 33, 64, 74, 143, 155
Korneichuk, Aleksandr (former secretary of Writers' Union), 97, 105, 110
Kosolapov, V. A. (former editor of Literaturnaya Gazeta), 56
Kosygin, Alexei (Premier), 119
Kozhevnikov, Aleksandr (Party secretary, Riazan), 143, 148, 153
Kozhevnikov, Vadim (author), 56, 105
Kravchenko, Viktor (Soviet deserter), 11
Kruzhkov, N. L. (critic), 49
Kuprin, Aleksandr (author), 7
Kuznetsov, Anatoli (author, exiled), 142, 146, 148

Lakshin, Vladimir (critic), 63, 64
Lazutin, I. (author), 61
Lenin, Vladimir Ilyich, 1, 15, 142
Lermontov, Mikhail (classic), 15
Levchenko, Nilolai (author), 146
Liberman, Yevsei (economist), 3
Licko, Pavel (Slovakian author), 11, 20, 22–41, 74, 133, 138, 156
Litvinov, Vasily (critic), 49
Louis, Victor (Soviet journalist), 73, 74, 124, 125, 127, 133, 137–140
Lugovskoi, Vladimir (poet), 7

Lunacharsky, Anatoli (Commissar under Lenin), 3
Lundkvist, Artur (Swedish author, member of the Swedish Academy), 94, 169
Lysenko, Trofim (geneticist), 31, 76

Mayakovsky, Vladimir (poet), 1, 3, 7, 89
Maltsev, Yelisar (author), 85
Mandelshtam, Osip (poet), 3, 89, 91
Markin, Yevgeni (author), 145
Markov, Georgi (Secretary of the Writers' Union), 94, 109, 117, 131
Marshak, Samuil (poet), 8, 63, 117
Martur (chemist), 31
Marx, Karl, 107
Masherov, Pyotr (Belorussian Party leader), 80
Matushkin, Vasily (author), 143–153
Mednikov, A., 84
Medvedev, Zhorez (Jaures) (gerontologist), 31, 74, 161, 162
Melentiev (Central Committee official), 96
Melnikov (former Captain), 24, 40
Meyerhold, Vsevolod (theater director, 1, 7, 53
Mikhoels, Solomon (actor, theater director), 1
Mihajlov, Mihajlo (Yugoslavian publicist), 64
Molotov, Vyacheslav (Stalinist politician), 2
Morits, Yunna (poet), 93
Musrepov, Gabit (Secretary of Writers' Union), 99

Neizvestny, Ernst (sculptor), 5, 6, 13, 50, 52
Nekrasov, Viktor (author), 5, 58, 151
Nekrich, Aleksandr (war historian), 29
Novichenko, Leonid (Secretary of the Writers' Union), 109
Novotny, Antonin (former Party leader in Czechoslovakia), 67

Okudzhava, Bulat (poet), 6, 87, 93, 143

Olyesha, Yuri (author), 7
Ozerov, Vitali (Secretary of the Writers' Union), 106

Pasternak, Boris (poet, Nobel laureate), 3, 7, 89, 107, 138, 155, 167
Paustovsky, Konstantin (author), 6, 93
Pavlov, Sergei (former First Secretary of Komsomol), 57, 65
Pilnyak, Boris (author), 3, 89
Platonov, Andrei (author), 7, 89
Polevoi, Boris (author, editor of Yunost), 8, 56
Poltoratsky, Viktor (author), 58
Poskriobyshev, Aleksandr (head of Stalin's Secretariat), 108
Potiomkin (lecturer), 98
Povaryonkin (editor), 143, 146
Pushkin, Alexandr (play-wright & novelist), 17, 89

Remizov, Alexei (author), 89
Reshetovskaya, Natalya (Solzhenitsyn's first wife), 20, 29, 40, 75–77
Riurikov, Boris (critic), 107–111
Rodin, Nikolai (author), 144
Rokossovsky, Konstantin (Marshal), 107
Romanov, Alexei (head of the state Movie Committee), 57
Romm, Mikhail (movie director), 54
Rostropovich, Mstislav (cellist), 162–167
Rozhdestvensky, Robert (poet), 5, 7, 13
Rozov, Viktor (dramatist), 8
Ruchov, Boris (poet), 65

Safonov, Ernst (Secretary of the Writers' Union of Riazan), 143
Saltykov-Shchedrin (author), 84
Salynsky, Afanasi (Secretary of the Writers' Union), 97
Samsonov, Aleksandr (Czarist General), 22
Sarnov, V. (author), 85
Sartakov, Sergei (Secretary of the Writers' Union), 94
Sazhin, R. (author), 85
Seliverstov, N. (critic), 61
Semenov, N. A. (energy specialist), 31
Semenov, Nikolai (chemist, Nobel laureate), 53

Semichastny, Vladimir (former head of the KGB), 102, 157
Sergeyev-Tsensky, Sergei (author), 106
Sergovantsev, N. (critic), 59
Shapiro, Henry (American journalist), 59
Sharipov, Adi (Secretary of the Writers' Union), 99
Shchipachov, Stepan (poet), 7
Shelest, Georgi (author), 55
Shelest, Pyotr (former Ukranian Party leader), 119
Shestakov (Major), 101
Sholokhov, Mikhail (author, Nobel laureate), 16, 54, 155
Shostakovich, Dimitri (composer), 54
Simonyan (unidentified), 29, 40
Simonyants (unidentified), 29, 40
Simonov, Konstantin (Secretary of the Writers' Union), 29, 53, 103
Sinyavsky, Andrei (author; in 1966 sentenced to 7 years, with hard labor for smuggling manuscripts), 79, 138, 157
Slavin, Lev (author), 84
Slutsky, Boris (poet), 6, 51, 93
Sobolev, Leonid (Secretary of the Writers' Union), 94
Sokolov, Mikhail (author), 58
Soloukhin, Vladimir (author), 93
Solzhenitsyn, Isai (Solzhenitsyn's father), 15
Solzhenitsyn, Taisya (Solzhenitsyn's mother), 15
Stalin, Joseph, 2, 108, 152
Strada, Vittorio (Italian publicist), 149
Surkov, Alexei (author), 105
Surov, A. (dramatist), 19
Svirsky, Grigori (author), 117

Tabidze, Tizian (author), 91
Tager, Yelena (author), 85
Tamm, Igor (Nobel laureate), 53
Tarkovsky, Arseni (author), 93
Tarsis, Valeri (author), 125
Tatlin, Vladimir (painter), 1, 3
Taurin, Frants (Secretary of RSFSR's Writers' Union), 143
Tendryakov, Vladimir (author), 93
Terekhov (Military Chief Prosecutor), 39
Teush (mathematician), 73, 130
Timofeyev-Resovsky, Nikolai (geneticist), 31, 77

Todorsky, Aleksandr (author, General), 64
Tolstoy, Leo (Lev), (novelist), 6, 84, 151
Travkin (Major General), 22
Tsvetaeva, Marina (poet), 6, 89, 90
Turchin, Valentin (writer), 128
Tvardovsky, Aleksandr (poet, former editor of Novy Mir), 9, 43, 58, 62, 64, 113–118

Vakhtangov, Yevgeni (theater director), 19
Vasilev, Pavel (poet), 91
Vesely, Artem (poet), 91
Vinnichenko, I., 84
Vitkevich, N. D. (Solzhenitsyn's childhood friend), 28, 40
Vladimov, Georgi (author), 94
Vlasov, Andrei (General, deserted to the Germans), 130
Voinovich, Vladimin (author), 58
Voitinskaya, Olga (author), 86
Voloshin, Maximilian (author), 89
Voronkov, Konstantin (Secretary of the Writers' Union), 94, 117, 131
Voroshilov, Kliment (Marshal), 2
Voznesensky, Andrei (poet), 5, 7, 51, 114

Yagoda, G. (head of KGB, executed in 1938), 91
Yashen, Kamil (Secretary of the Writers' Union), 109
Yashin, Aleksandr (author), 58
Yegorychev, Nikolai (Party secretary of Moscow), 80
Yeremin, Dmitri (author), 64
Yermilov, Viktor (critic), 49
Yesenin, Sergei (poet), 7, 89, 114
Yevtushenko, Yevgeni (poet), 1, 5, 7, 8, 49–57, 114
Yezhov, Nicolai (head of KGB, executed in 1939), 91

Zabolotsky, Nikolai (poet), 7, 91
Zamyatin, Yevgeni (author), 89, 106
Zavadsky, Yuri (theater director), 19, 53
Zimyanin, Mikhail (editor of Pravda), 114, 138
Zoshchenko, Mikhail (author), 7, 90